Activate Your RAS

The Art and Science of Creating Your Reality
from the Inside Out

Sian Hill

Contents

Foreword

Please allow me to introduce myself. My name is David Shephard. I'm just a boy from Mansfield, a small mining town in Nottinghamshire, who dreamed of being the next Elvis.

After a successful career in the City Of London, in 1990 I was introduced to these things called Neuro Linguistic Programming (NLP) and spiritual development. WOW! This stuff blew my mind. I devoured books by Anthony Robbins, Richard Bandler, John Grinder, Dan Millman, Stuart Wilde and myriad others.

In 1993 I decided I wanted to get serious and make this a way of life and business. I trained in NLP, Hypnosis, Time Line Therapy® and Hawaiian Huna. I founded The Performance Partnership in the UK in 1993.

I say all of this because that is how I met Sian Hill, a few years ago, and what makes this foreword meaningful.

In *Activate Your RAS*, Sian has created a first, certainly, in the book world. It's structured so that you can binge read it or do ten minutes throughout your day, whether that's between looking after your family or during your daily commute.

Sian has integrated, expertly, a number of my passions – The Seven Hermetic Laws from *The Kybalion*, NLP, neuroscience and Magic – so that you won't need to have the thousands of books I have in my library. In just one book, Sian has expertly distilled the essence of all these things.

There is a saying that, in theory, there is little difference between theory and practice; and, in practice, there is a huge difference between theory and practice. Sian handles that masterfully with practical application of the theories explained in each chapter and step-by-step exercises.

I know that what Sian teaches in *Activate Your RAS* works. Read the book, do the exercises and get your RAS in gear. When you do that, no more excuses!

Best Wishes All Ways,

David Shephard

Master Trainer of NLP
Master Trainer of Time Line Therapy®
Master Trainer of Hypnosis
Master Trainer of NLP Coaching
Kumu Huna

www.performancepartnership.com
www.c21nlp.com
www.facebook.com/thedavidshephard
www.linkedin.com/in/nlpdavidshephard
www.instagram.com/nlpdavidshephard

Introduction

The best way to foresee the story is to write it.

It was just another Thursday afternoon. There was nothing out of the ordinary happening, except for the red car. It seemed to be following me. The funny thing was, I'd never noticed it before and yet now it was everywhere. I had to wonder whether it had always been there.

I'd only thought about the red car for the first time the day before and suddenly it was appearing on every street corner, every driveway, even the supermarket car park. What on earth was going on?

Let me backtrack slightly to the previous week when I was first introduced to the concept that us humans have the ability to create our own realities. By 'creating our own realities', I mean that no matter what we wanted – big or small – we could achieve it. This was something I'd had no idea about and it was big news. I was very excited at the possibility that it could be true and keen to know how, so I could get started straightaway. There was a backlog of things I wanted to create, so I had some catching up to do. My understanding from the little I had read was that our thoughts become things, so all I had to do was ask the universe to deliver what I wanted, imagine the life I desired in my mind and trust it would arrive. Simple. I kick-started my creation process by doing just that.

I let my imagination wander as I thought about the shiny new red car I'd been drooling over. I pictured myself driving it, my hands on the steering wheel whilst I sang along to my favourite songs with the windows down and feeling pretty cool. It was only a few days later that something odd began happening. That very car, the one I thought was unique, seemed to be everywhere I turned and I'm not just talking about on the roads: it was in magazines and TV adverts; I even saw it in the background of people's Facebook posts. It was the strangest thing and whilst it was exciting, I had no idea what it really meant.

Was it a sign?

Was I on the right track to receiving the car?

I wondered if I should just carry on imagining it and trust that things would fall into place when the time was right.

I wasn't sure whether to go with the flow and just believe the car would land on my driveway.

I found myself asking the universe if it was telling me that I should just go for it – take out a loan and hope I'd have the money for the repayments when they were due.

I felt excited but confused, hopeful but frustrated, eager but overwhelmed, happy when I saw the car, sad that I didn't have one and a whole mixture of emotions in-between!! What I really wanted to know was...

WHAT WAS THE SHINY RED CAR TELLING ME?

Sound familiar? Of course, this isn't just limited to cars.

When I first found out that I could create my own reality, I took everything as a sign. I would play a song I loved for the first time in years and it then seemed to be playing everywhere I went – in shops, bars, on the radio – and it wasn't even popular. I investigated the words in the song to see if there was a message within the lyrics that I needed to know.

After really enjoying a certain brand of peanut butter at a friend's house and wanting some for myself, there it was on the shelf in every supermarket and every corner shop I entered. It appeared on adverts, billboards, leaflets, but I could've sworn it hadn't existed before the first day I put it on my toast.

I decided to get a cat and to no surprise, my cat, or at least a very close lookalike, lived across the street, down the road, on the front of cat food and some of them even had the same name. I couldn't help but question how I had not seen them before.

Were they always there? If that was the case, how had I not noticed them?

I had so many questions around the idea of being able to create my own reality and what that had to do with the things I'd been thinking about showing up everywhere I went.

My initial introduction into this world came through a book that wrote about the universal law known as the Law of Attraction.

The Law of Attraction states that like attracts like; thoughts become things and you can manifest anything you want. 'Manifest' simply means to bring something into existence. The basic concept is that we emit energy, and all energy has a certain energetic frequency to it that vibrates at a certain rate. Just like magnets, when frequencies are a vibrational match, they attract each other. When our thoughts are a match to the things we desire, they become our reality and so you get what you think about. It made sense. I'd thought about all of those things – the car, the song, the peanut butter, the cat and its name – and so there they were, showing up everywhere, although not necessarily on my driveway!

Back to my earlier question, what did those things showing up actually mean?

After lots of reading and research on the subject, I came to the conclusion that I must be on track to creating the things I wanted in my life, because I was surrounded by them. I was sure it was evidence that I was on my way to being a vibrational match, otherwise why else would I be seeing them? It was a sign!

From the little knowledge I had at that point, I decided that when the things I desired randomly showed up a number of times – things I'd never really noticed until I wanted them for myself – it was the universe telling me to go for it, whatever 'it' was. When I say, 'go for it', let me be clear: what that often meant was buying the things I wanted to create in my life, even when I couldn't afford them. I believed that even though it felt scary and I had my doubts, I should take the plunge. Feel the fear and do it anyway! The universe had shown me that I was vibrationally aligned with my desires, because I was seeing them all over the place, so I just needed to trust in the process and believe it would all be ok.

It didn't turn out to be quite that simple and I very quickly discovered there was a difference between stepping outside of what felt comfortable, trusting that everything would work out and putting myself in a position that was doomed to fail from the start.

The reality was that when I first started reading about how thoughts become things, I barely had the money to eat, let alone treat myself to the car I had been eyeing up that was way out of my price range. I had gone on to read a number of books soon after learning about the Law of Attraction and they all said the same thing: if I could see it in my mind, then I could have it. I pictured money rolling into my bank account every day. I imagined the shiny red car I wanted landing on my driveway. The man of my dreams arriving on a white horse to come and rescue me. My dream job being offered to me out of nowhere.

It turned out that just trusting money would appear, whilst simultaneously losing sleep over my ever-growing list of bills, didn't actually work in the way I'd hoped! But I was stubborn and wanted to prove I could do it, that visualising the life I wanted would bring it into my experience, and so I persevered. It took me a while to recognise there was more than just imagination required to pay for the material things I wanted. Whilst I believed anything was possible, that logic didn't necessarily apply to me and I managed to get myself into debt at an impressive rate. The lack of belief I had in my ability to create the life I wanted very quickly became a never-ending cycle of negativity that kept feeding itself. A cycle that I couldn't seem to find a way out of.

I tried visualising and it didn't work, which proved that I was a failure...

I believed I was a failure, so I behaved like a failure...

Behaving like a failure led to results of failing...

I proved myself right... Aha! I thought I was a failure and I was right!

Round and round the cycle went with what felt like no exit point in sight. The more I thought it, the more evidence I gathered that it was true, making the belief stronger every time.

What it did show me was that our thoughts really do become things.

After many months of sitting at home, taking little action and hoping my lottery ticket would come in (I hate to be the bearer of bad news – that doesn't work), I was so frustrated and decided I'd had enough of lounging around and thinking. It was time to take action. Even so, the desires I had were much bigger than my belief that I could achieve them, and looking back, I can see the amount of action I took was a reflection of that belief... in other words, very little! There was an obvious mismatch between what I wanted and what I thought was even probable, let alone likely.

So, back to the question, what is the shiny red car, or any other object of your desire, trying to tell you? What does it mean?

I have some good news, there is a simple answer to why the very things you long for and repeatedly think about begin to show up time and time again in your experience. It's all to do with your RAS, or your reticular activating system, to give it its fullest name.

Meet Your RAS

Let me introduce you... (I'll keep the science brief for now!)

Your RAS is a small piece of the brain that sits close to the top of the spinal column, extending upwards about two inches, with a diameter the size of a pencil. And in that piece of the brain is a whole bundle of nerves.

All of your senses – everything you see, hear, feel and taste – are wired to the neurons in that bundle; everything that is, except for your sense of smell, which goes to your emotional centre. There is so much information being received through your senses every second of the day, far too much for you to consciously process and be aware of. Your RAS acts like a radar, scanning everything around you, all of the sensory information you are taking in, and it filters through it and decides which bits are important and which bits are not. The things your RAS deems important are the things you are then aware of. It activates and sends a signal to your conscious mind, bringing that very thing to your attention. The things that are not deemed important aren't brought to your attention; they are unknowingly left out of your awareness.

Your RAS is essentially the gatekeeper of your conscious mind!

The red car had been mentally labelled as important and so my RAS had allowed it through and alerted me of its existence.

The reason it's such a huge part in creating your reality, and the reason it's a good idea to become acquainted with your RAS, is because there are opportunities metaphorically knocking on your door every day, but if your RAS isn't on high alert and activated when those opportunities are ready and waiting, then you simply won't know they even exist.

So, the real questions are, how does your RAS know when to activate? What do you do with that information? And how do you change its signal if your activation is not on target to achieving your goals?

This book is going to explain just that!

To set the tone for what we'll cover, it's important to first mention that the reality you know isn't actually reality at all. It's only your perception of it which, ironically, is therefore your reality. Now, saying this is all very well and good but if you're anything like me, you're probably wondering what it really means and, more importantly, what can you do about it?

There's an old saying, dating back centuries, from the Greek god Hermes Trismegistus:

"As within, so without."

This statement is very true. You really do create your reality from the inside out, which means you do indeed have the ability to purposefully create your life. Powerful stuff, right? Of course, only when you know how to change your internal world that is!

There is another saying:

"Knowledge is power."

Also true. Well, it's half the story anyway. Knowledge does indeed have the potential to be powerful but it only goes so far. Knowing something isn't the same as doing it and the real power lies in the application of the knowledge.

Let's face it, everyone knows that eating well and regular exercise are a big part of what makes you physically healthy but knowing this doesn't change anything unless you use that knowledge to take action. Yet, without that knowledge, where would you begin? It's the same when it comes to turning your dreams into your reality.

This book will take you on a journey into your mind. You will learn the mechanics of creation, which is the first step in understanding how to apply it in your own life through the practical tips and exercises. Full disclaimer: be prepared to discover a great deal about yourself and, by default, you'll learn about others too, which will probably answer a lot of questions you have about some people along the way. It certainly did for me!

Before you dive in, here's a quick guide on how to use this book.

As with anything in life, there are always exceptions, so if I generalise at points throughout this book, it's only to assist in understanding the message I want to get across.

I'm assuming that because you are reading this, you are ready to begin making changes in your life. For change to happen, you have to know where you are starting from.

You are going to learn a lot about yourself and other people through this process; maybe you will recognise elements of yourself in some of the stories you read.

This book is filled with lots of interesting information about the process of creation and manifestation. Throughout this book, you will also find Activation Points, which are practical tips and exercises to put your knowledge into action and begin making positive changes in your life.

My suggestion is to read the book from beginning to end and in order, as each chapter builds on the previous one and so jumping ahead may leave you a little confused.

You can carry out the exercises as you go along, or you may prefer to read through the whole book first and then revisit the exercises in the order they appear in the book.

The best way to get results from the exercises is to answer the questions from the heart, trusting whatever comes to mind.

Allow yourself to be vulnerable and uncover some of the things that you may have been unaware of until reading this book. If you hold back, then the things you want in life will hold back too.

You can use this book as a working manual and refer back to any chapter and the Activation Points in them, as needed in the future.

Most importantly, enjoy this part of the never-ending journey of self-discovery and growth.

You may be wondering who I am and why you should listen to anything I have to say. Now is probably a good time to introduce myself. Hey, I'm Sian, an internationally certified trainer of neuro linguistic programming, Time Line Therapy®, hypnotherapy and a master coach.

Having been in a position where not waking up seemed like the better option, right the way through to today where, whilst I do love my bed, I only wish now that I could survive with less sleep so I could spend more time awake and doing the things I love!

After much frustration on my journey of personal development, I stumbled across tools and techniques that changed my life in so many ways. I have achieved things that, in the past, would've seemed impossible (writing this book being one of them). Much of what I talk about in this book is based on the models that I have learnt over a decade of my own learning.

Although I can't include everything I have learnt in one book, I have personally used everything I'll be sharing with you. If you take just one thing from this book that changes your perception, that could be enough to change the whole trajectory of your life!

It's important to say here that I am still on a journey of growth, of becoming and stepping into the person I need to be so I can do and have everything I want in life. I used to beat myself up for not having already achieved all of my goals and being at the metaphorical finish line. I've now come to appreciate that it's a journey that never ends; there is always more! This really is a good thing – imagine if you reached the peak of your existence and that was it! Then what?

I consider myself to be a student of life, always ready to learn. I invite you to join me. To come along and share this experience of personal growth together. Through the ups and downs, the highs and lows, knowing there is always something for us to learn and that we are never done.

My intention in writing this book is to help you live a life you feel excited to wake up to every morning. A life that, even with its ups and downs (side note: you will still have those), gives you the passion to keep going, to reach for your big goals and know they are possible. I want you to understand yourself a little more, as well as the things that have led you here today and how to take steps to create the tomorrow you've been dreaming of.

All I ask is that you read this book with an open mind and heart, knowing that, like any book, it's certainly not a magic pill that will make everything you don't want disappear, nor will a shiny red car manifest itself onto your driveway tomorrow. What it will do is help you understand how you really can make big changes through learning and applying the art and science of creating your reality.

With that in mind, let's begin!

Chapter 1
Physical Creation

To be unstoppable, you must know, feel, think and take action.

First things first, if you want to create physical manifestations in your life, understanding where the physical fits into the equation of this thing we call reality is of huge importance.

There are many differing models and schools of thought around this topic, and in an effort to keep things simple, I'll be sharing a brief summary of what I believe is relevant to understand the basics of how we mould the world around us.

The universe consists of four planes of existence, which contribute to the lives we live – be that intentionally or unintentionally. When creating any change, all four planes need to be taken into consideration and tended to in order to create alignment. The planes are spiritual, mental, emotional, and physical. Each has its place in your experience of the universe, individually and collectively.

The Spiritual Plane

The term 'spiritual' in this context is simply a representation of the higher-self. The higher-self is *everything*; it's bigger than just us as physical human beings. It encompasses and knows all things and so all of creation happens on this plane. It's often referred to as infinite intelligence or the universe.

The Mental Plane

The mental plane is where your conscious mind resides, which is your thinking mind. The mental plane is the birthplace of what you want. You consciously set an intention to create something that doesn't currently exist in physical form. It's a powerful gateway to creation through intentional focus. It has the ability to keep us grounded through its rational perspective.

The Emotional Plane

The emotional plane is the home of your unconscious mind. It's the way you feel in any moment, be that an emotion you would call positive or negative, good or bad; either way, those emotions are all generated from your unconscious mind. The feelings we have about ourselves, others, the world, our situation and everything in it all exist on the emotional plane. In terms of creation, the emotional plane is where the energy needed for physical manifestation is generated.

The Physical Plane

The physical plane is exactly that. It's the tangible existence where much of creation is evident in its physical form. Think of everything around you, from your house, car, shoes, phone, couch, plant pot, body, this book… everything you can physically grasp.

To relate this model to the process of manifestation, it starts with the conscious mind when you decide that you want something. The unconscious mind is responsible for the emotion behind it, the energy that creates it. On the spiritual plane of your higher-self, the part of you that is all-knowing and connected to everything, the manifestation is already done. There is a delay in that energy taking physical form which we will cover in more detail later on in the book.

In my experience, I've noticed that people will spend the majority of their time focused or working on one plane more than the others, sometimes even discounting the others completely. The reason it's important to acknowledge the existence of all four planes is because no plane is good or bad, wrong or right, better or worse than any other plane. They each have their purpose and in the process of building your ideal life, taking all planes into account is fundamental to the results you get. Without doing so, issues can often arise, because people spend time working on the wrong plane, particularly when attempting to solve a problem. I use the word 'wrong' to make a point because, as I mentioned, no single plane is wrong or right. That being said, when a problem occurs or change is desired, it exists on a specific plane and so it has to be resolved on the plane that it is created on.

Think of it like this: if someone has problems that are physical, such as issues with money or a lack of energy from a poor diet and little sleep, first of all, they need to focus on the physical plane to make any necessary changes.

Whilst the planes are all linked and all influence each other, it's important to identify which plane a problem originates from and, therefore, where it needs to be resolved whilst, at the same time, making sure the other planes are in alignment

Hence why all planes are both individual and a collective at the same time.

I spent years trying to change the physical things in my life through thought alone. Money was a big issue for me at the time and so I repeated the affirmation *"I attract money easily"* at least 200 times a day. The problems I was experiencing were overdue fees on my credit card, debtors sending final demands and very little money to survive on day to day. Unfortunately, no amount of meditating was going to pay the bills. The immediate problem was a physical one; it existed on the physical plane and required physical action. In other words, picking up the phone and arranging a payment plan and getting work to pay the bills.

That was the starting point, but the other planes also required attention to make sure the action I did take was forward-focused (mental) and positive rather than fear-driven (emotional) – more to come on that later. This principle is the same across all planes.

A common example, and one I've witnessed all too often, is amazing people who have lost weight, bought new clothes and got haircuts in the hope they will feel good about themselves, only to find they are the same people they were before they made the physical changes. They still have the same thoughts and feelings about themselves. They made changes on the outside, on the physical plane, but didn't work on the mental and emotional planes and so the inside stayed the same. Making changes that are considered physically desirable doesn't guarantee your thoughts and feelings will change too.

The spiritual plane, where your higher-self exists, is where faith and trust come in. You can take physical action, consciously think about what you want to achieve, unconsciously believe it will happen and even then, there are no guarantees. This is where you hand it over to a being that is bigger than all of that. Doing your part whilst, at the same time, letting the universe take care of the rest.

As we transcend and evolve through the different phases of life, there will always be a particular plane that requires more focus than the others. The key to becoming the captain of your life is to have all four planes in harmony with each other and working together!

ACTIVATION POINT – *The Plane of Existence*

Think about a change you want to make in your life or a problem you want to resolve.

Ask yourself the following questions:

- **Which plane does the root of this problem exist on?**
  - ◦ Spiritual (higher-self) – bigger than and including everyone and everything
  - ◦ Mental – thinking
  - ◦ Emotional – feelings
  - ◦ Physical – something tangible

For example,

Person A: *"I want to lose weight but I don't do any exercise and I often eat fast food because it's quick and easy."* (Physical)

Person B: *"I go to the gym and keep active but I eat to make me feel good."* (Emotional)

- **If I were to work on just one plane, which would have the biggest impact first?**

Person A: Physical

"Starting with this will have immediate results."

Person B: Emotional

"Dealing with my emotions will stop the overeating and the physical effort will begin to pay off."

Trying to change everything at once can very quickly become overwhelming, and the very thing that needs addressing can easily be overlooked. By identifying which plane the problem exists on, you can begin to break it down and deal with it, one step at a time. Working on the plane where the problem exists will usually have a positive knock-on effect on the other planes too.

Chapter 2
The Laws of Your Universe

"Take away the cause and the effect ceases."
Miguel de Cervantes

We are very soon going to be getting into the nitty-gritty of you and your RAS, but bear with me for just a little while longer first.

In the wonderful place we know as the universe, along with the four planes – physical, mental, emotional and spiritual – there are also seven primary natural laws, or principles, that act as a framework by which the universe operates. Understanding these laws, which planes they exist on and how you can utilise them is the foundation of your existence.

Of these seven universal laws, there are some that are much more well-known and spoken about than others. However, in isolation, much of their power is lost. These laws are present and happening at all times; you cannot turn them off or pick and choose which ones you will use and when. They all have an impact on your results and your ability to become an expert creator in your life, so understanding them is a key part of understanding you.

I won't be going into any great detail in this book; there are many resources you can find on this topic if you want to know more; I have listed some in the Resources section at the back of this book. However, you will become aware of the laws' existence and how you can purposefully use them to make positive changes in your life.

Let's explain the whole 'law' thing first. To keep it simple, everyone knows and accepts the Law of Gravity, right? What goes up, must come down. Knowing the Law of Gravity exists influences the way you behave and the choices you make. For example, you probably use the stairs rather than the second-floor bedroom window when leaving the house, because in knowing the Law of Gravity, you accept that the second-floor window option may not end well. It also gives you peace of mind that when a child jumps high in the air on a bouncy castle, you can sit and watch, safe in the knowledge that they will eventually come back down again.

What you need to be aware of here is that gravity is neither good nor bad, and the same is true for everything else in life. Nothing that exists is good or bad, nor does it have any meaning unless you give it meaning. Assuming you can defy the laws is like throwing an apple in the air and hoping it will never come back down again. If you're not careful, you may well get hit in the face by a falling apple… Better to use your knowledge and the laws to your advantage and work in harmony with them!

Immutable or mutable? That is the question…

Each law falls into one of two categories: immutable or mutable.

Sounds fancy, right?

The immutable laws are the first three laws and, quite simply, they are laws that are fixed – they cannot be changed.

The mutable laws are the other four laws and these laws can be changed or transcended.

Immutable Laws	Mutable Laws
Law of Mentalism	Law of Polarity
Law of Correspondence	Law of Rhythm
Law of Vibration	Law of Cause and Effect
	Law of Gender

The principles all link and work together to create this thing we call life. Learning the basics will give you some insight, not only into yourself but also the bigger picture at play and the impact it has on you personally.

Immutable Laws

Law #1: Law of Mentalism

"The universe is mental, held in the mind of THE ALL."

Put another way, the mind is all; the universe is mental!

The universe is the source of all things and those 'things' include you. ALL is everything that exists, everything you could ever think of, the universe itself… I mean *everything*. Every single one of us is born from the same one source, which means we all have that source within us.

The 'all' literally contains everything and so nothing exists outside of it, before it or after it. It is the whole, so you are part of the universe and the universe is part of you.

The law states that the mind is all, which means that everything that is created is also your mind.

Stick with me here!

The universe is mental, so therefore everything is created through the mind. Every single thing that ever has or ever will exist starts and is experienced in the mind first.

Your physical reality is a reflection of your mental reality.

If the whole universe is mental, then reality is not an external experience – it's all internal. In other words, your reality exists in your mind and you can create your own experience of it. This also means you are the only one who can change it. Now that may sound a bit scary: *"Oh crap! I'm in charge of my entire life"*.

Well, here's the thing… Because you are the only one in control of your reality, that means you're already doing it, so you may as well do it on purpose!

Your entire existence all happens through your mind, so anything you have the capacity to think, you also have the ability to create… Starting to sound more like fun?

The thing that stops people from doing just that are their beliefs, emotions and perceptions of what something is.

> *"All things exist, but man knows of them only so far*
> *as he is educated to comprehend them.*
> *What is a fact to one is an unreality to another;*
> *thus, no two people will exactly agree upon a given subject."*
> The Law of Mentalism – A. Victor Segno, 1902

Think of it like this: we can all agree that rain, in and of itself, has no meaning. Yet, to a farmer, it could fill them with joy knowing their crops will be watered. A small child, on the other hand, could be sad because they can no longer go out to play at the park.

There is no good or bad in life; it's all about perspective!

The mind creates everything and you are part of everything, so you have the power to do, be or have anything. There is no physical path that isn't first born in the mind. This is where the energy is created – in the mental.

Slightly mind-bending, hey?

The key point to all of this is to know that you are the one in control of your own mind! No one can make you think anything unless you choose to and understanding this is a great starting point to mastering your thoughts.

Everything that is created in the physical plane is mental first. Without a thought of a table, a table would not exist and therefore it would not be able to become a physical thing. The focus or intention of your observation changes your reality. If you're not focusing on something in your world, then does it even exist? Focus is powerful when it comes to choosing the direction of your life, so I highly recommend that you begin to become aware of what you are focusing on.

The joy of creation is being able to bring the thoughts from the mental plane into the physical plane. Many people resist this part as it's much easier to sit and think about what you want than it is to take action. The thing is, more often than not, people's desires are for something tangible – money, cars, houses, holidays and so on.

As with everything, there is, of course, the flip side to that, where people spend their whole time being physical, pursuing their lives with brute force, taking non-stop action without ever attending to what's happening on the mental plane, in their minds.

The mind is what creates the will to act (mental); action needs to then be taken (physical). Not tending to the mental can certainly make physical action feel like an uphill battle. When the mental is in alignment, the physical follows far more easily.

Use the Law of Mentalism to clear the mental path; create what you want mentally first. The Law of Mentalism allows you to zoom out your perspective and see that you are part of a much bigger picture and so much more connected and powerful than you know.

ACTIVATION POINT – *Applying the Law of Mentalism*

Begin to become aware of your thoughts and notice any limiting beliefs or negative emotions you have that could prevent you from achieving what you want.

You can use the following questions as prompts:

- **What beliefs do I have that could prevent me from creating the life I desire?**
- **What emotions are present when I think about the things I want and the beliefs associated with them?**

Write down whatever comes to mind, even if it doesn't make any sense at this point.

Once completed, go through each belief and emotion and ask yourself the following questions:

- **How would I know if that belief wasn't true? What would have to happen?**
- **If the emotion disappeared right now, what did I learn from the events that created it?**

Just considering these questions will begin to turn you towards overcoming those obstacles. Good job!

Law #2: Law of Correspondence

"As above, so below. As within, so without."

The Law of Correspondence is the principle that you are totally in control of your reality.

Remember, we live in a world that exists on different planes: the physical plane, which is matter (the earth-bound stuff); then there is the mental plane, which is your mind and consciousness; the emotional plane, which is your unconscious mind; and finally, the spiritual plane, which is where you have access to your higher consciousness.

There is a correspondence between each of the planes, which means the experiences that you have on one plane are a direct reflection of what is happening on the other planes too. There is nothing in your external experience that isn't happening in your internal experience – the planes are a mirror image of each other.

If a change takes place on the physical plane, there must also be a change happening on the mental plane. If you shift the physical, there has to be a shift on the mental, as they correspond with each other; they are both evolving at the same time.

To bring this to life, imagine we have Person A and Person B. Person A wants to do good and *"save the world"*, whereas Person B prefers to spend their time complaining about how rubbish the world is and everything in it. As someone looking in, you would probably assume the internal worlds of Person A and Person B are very different, and they will be because no two people ever have the same experience of the world, but either way, both people see the world as being broken in some form. They both see a world that needs fixing, improving or saving.

If we apply the Law of Correspondence to this situation, when someone sees the world as needing to be saved or fixed, this will be a reflection of what is happening internally for that person. It may be that they feel broken in some way or like they need saving.

The way to change how you see the world and to really save it is to save yourself, because everything is a reflection of you. What is happening on the inside, your thoughts and feelings, is what determines everything outside of you. Remember, this works both ways as each plane corresponds with the others. When the things you take in from the outside change, the inside will also change, so start to become mindful of how you spend your time and who you spend it with.

Be aware of what you feed your body, the physical part of you, as it will always impact on the other planes. This also applies to what you feed your mind and your spirit which, of course, correspond with your physical experience. What happens on one plane also happens on the 'ALL'.

You are part of the universe (the above), and the universe is within you (the below).

The Law of Correspondence is such an important law and it links the three immutable laws together.

ACTIVATION POINT – *Applying the Law of Correspondence*

Begin to use your experience of your external reality as feedback by reflecting it back on yourself. This relates to both the wanted and the unwanted.

If there is something you want to change, ask yourself the following questions and just trust what comes to mind.

- **What is it within me that's causing this external experience?**

Notice the words you use and turn them inwards.

If the world outside of you is filled with lack, scarcity or helplessness, then ask where in yourself you feel those things.

- **What do I need to change in me so the reflection outside of me changes?**

Remember, the outside is a reflection of you and you are a reflection of it. When you know the cause of your life events, you can choose whether or not you want to change them.

- **What am I feeding myself, mentally and physically?**

Our physical behaviour can often fall out of our awareness and without us even noticing. This could include the food you eat, exercise, sleep, meditation, relaxation, relationships, who you spend your time with, the activities you do, TV shows you watch, books you read, conversations you have… and any other areas that affect your mental and physical well-being.

Make a note of how you spend your time and with whom, and notice how you feel when you do. If something, or someone, isn't serving you, maybe it's time to let it go.

- **What positive changes can I make to my body and mind?**

Decide what you will do instead. Making small changes adds up to big changes over time. Pick one or two and do those first before starting on the next. The small wins will soon build up.

This is exciting! Trying to change the world never works – there are too many things outside of your control. The only thing you can change is you, and when you do, the world you see will change.

"Be the change you wish to see in the world."
Gandhi

Law #3: Law of Vibration

"Nothing rests, everything moves, everything vibrates."
"Energy is everything and everything is energy."

This is the language of energy and the basis of the Law of Attraction, which is a secondary law because vibration is what causes attraction. The Law of Vibration states that everything that exists is vibrating; nothing stands still. Whilst this may not appear to be the case when you're looking at a pretty sturdy table, if you were to put that table under a microscope (albeit a very big one), you would indeed see that it is actually moving.

So, energy is the core of absolutely everything, even things that appear solid. That very sturdy table is vibrating at a frequency that makes it appear to you in the form that it does. Scientists believe that all things in the universe are made of particles, which are exceptionally small pieces of matter. Those particles are energy travelling in wave form and the up-and-down sequence of each wave varies. The variation is what determines the objects that you perceive in front of you. Whilst you can't see particles vibrating, they are the very things keeping the sturdy items that you can touch in place.

Think about it like a guitar string being plucked. The frequency at which the string vibrates determines the sounds that are produced; this is the same for all matter and physical creation.

The frequency of the vibration is the only difference between our physical body and the 'ALL'. Matter has a lower frequency, so the more solid something is, the slower the particles are moving and the slower the speed or rate of vibration. The faster the vibration of the particles, the more energy-based and less tangible the physical form.

The frequency at which something vibrates is the number of wave cycles per second. Because everything is energy, there is no difference between you and the material stuff outside of you; it's just a different frequency. Changing the frequency of vibration changes the experience in the physical form. As humans, we are also vibrating, constantly. The only variable is the rate we vibrate at, which is determined by how we feel. When you feel good, the frequency you vibrate at increases and so physical manifestations happen more quickly (more to come on that later on).

The physical world is focused thought, focused vibration, and this is true of you too. Everything that exists in the physical began as a thought. The more focus you give to a thought, whether positive or negative, the more focused it becomes and it then matches the experiences, the people and the physical-form manifestations that are equal to it. You can be in your physical body and be a vibrational match to things that have not yet made their way into your experience, but they are coming!

Remember, the Law of Correspondence states that if things change on one plane, the other planes must correspond to and be a reflection of that. If there are changes to your vibration on the mental and emotional plane, the physical plane must correspond. Now, there is a time lag between the mental and the physical, so whilst the things you think about may not immediately fall out of the sky, they are in the formation process. Think of it like the birth of a baby. No one expects a baby to be ready to go after three months of pregnancy. There is a nine-month gestation period, when the baby is making its way into the physical form. Whilst there is no set timeframe for a manifestation to make its way into your world, there is a gestation period where the energy is taking form and so the same law applies.

The question is, how can you increase your rate of vibration so you can start matching it to the things you desire?

And, how long do you have to wait before the metaphorical baby is born, before thoughts become things?

We'll get to that soon! To truly be a purposeful creator of your reality, you need to understand how it works first!

ACTIVATION POINT – *Applying the Law of Vibration*

You're already becoming aware of your thoughts through your application of the Law of Mentalism. It's time to take it a step further.

Your thoughts influence the way you feel.

- **Notice the feelings that are associated to thoughts you have – how do the thoughts feel?**

- **When you have a good feeling out of the blue, become aware of what you were thinking about?**

By this point, you will have identified some thoughts that feel good and some that don't feel so good.

- **Make a decision to focus daily on the 'good feeling' thoughts.**

   Take just a few minutes a day to sit and really get into the detail of each thought. Become aware of what you can see in your mind, what sounds are present, the feelings, smells or tastes. As you notice all of those finer details, allow the good feelings to become more intense. Then, allow these feelings to spread throughout your body.

Start with just a few minutes and if you want to, stay there longer. This exercise should be fun, so do it for the sheer pleasure of it and enjoy the process!

To summarise the immutable, unchangeable laws:

1. The Law of Mentalism

The mind is the 'ALL'; the universe is mental (the mind), so therefore you are everything and everything is you.

2. The Law of Correspondence

You are the 'ALL' and the 'ALL' is everything, so the four planes of existence – physical, mental, emotional and spiritual – that make up your being, are all one. When one changes, the others must correspond.

3. The Law of Vibration

Everything is energy and vibrates at a certain frequency. The universe is mental and you are part of it. Your thoughts and feelings emit at a frequency rate that dictates the physical things that show up outside of you. As your internal frequency changes, so does your external reality. You are in the 'ALL' and the physical manifestation must correspond.

Mutable Laws

Law #4: Law of Polarity

"Everything exists in duality, everything has poles, everything has its opposite. However, opposites are identical in their nature and different only in degree."

Everything is one thing that is expressed into two things: a positive and a negative, or a masculine and a feminine energy, although not necessarily related to gender. It's important to note that the word 'positive' in this context doesn't mean better; batteries have a positive and a negative charge that works together. When it comes to creation, there will always be something that is wanted and then its polar opposite, the unwanted.

For everything that exists, there will be an opposite end of the scale: light and dark, loud and quiet, rich and poor, happy and sad. Everything is dual.

To understand how two things are expressed as one, think about it in terms of hot and cold. Whilst hot and cold are opposites, they are also varying degrees of the same thing – temperature. This is where the saying, 'there is a thin line between love and hate' comes from; they're both on the same scale. The law is relative to each person – what you think of as being at one end of the pole, another person may see further down, as a lesser degree.

There is a duality in everything; opposites are an illusion!

There are two ends of everything – the wanted and the unwanted. If you focus on what you don't want, the opposite of what you desire at one end of the pole, then the other end of the pole – its opposite and what you do want – must exist; it's the law.

Although it may appear there are two opposites, it's really only one thing, so if you reject one end, you're inadvertently rejecting the other end too. If you reject not having enough money by moaning about it, looking for all the reasons why it is that way, blaming things outside of you, resenting those who have it, then you also reject extreme wealth.

Duality exists; therefore, you have to know the hardships in order for the positives to exist too. The polar opposite of what you want is where your desires are born.

Let's face it, there's nothing quite like a crappy relationship to make it very clear what you don't want! This is a great starting point for discovering the opposite, giving you clarity so you can begin to direct your focus.

ACTIVATION POINT – *Applying the Law of Polarity*

Start appreciating the experiences you have had to date, especially the ones that, until now, you may have seen as bad, pointless or a waste of time. Without them, you wouldn't be aware of their opposites.

Ask yourself the following questions:

- **What is the polar opposite of the things I don't want?**

  If you hate your job, the opposite could be a job you love or your own business that fulfils you, working with people you enjoy spending time with.

- **What does your life look, sound and feel like when you are living that experience? Write down your answer in as much detail as you can.**

  Do this exercise from a place of enjoyment. You now know the opposite end of the scale to where you currently, or don't want to, exist, so indulge in it. The mental plane corresponds with the physical, so start mentally creating the reality you desire.

There is one place where duality does not exist: the spiritual plane because on the spiritual plane everything is one. When you make the decision to rise above judgement or the labelling of things as being either good or bad – whether that's thoughts, feelings, people, circumstances or events – you don't become attached to either extreme of the scale. You're then able to see either side of any situation as being different expressions of the same thing.

Accepting where you are now as the gift it truly is, is the first step to creating its opposite. Polarity is the gift of clarity!

Law #5: Law of Rhythm

"Everything flows, everything has its tides, all things rise and fall, a pendulum that swings to the right swings to the left in equal measure, what goes up must come down, rhythm compensates."

The Law of Rhythm applies to everything in life. Waves that come in must go back out. Every day is followed by night and every night is followed by day. When there is a downfall in the economy, it's followed by a boom. These are the natural rhythms of life and for every high, there will be an equal low.

"The measure of the swing to the right is the measure
of the swing to the left; rhythm compensates."

We can use a pendulum to demonstrate how the law works: when it swings in one direction, by law it has to then swing back in the opposite direction to compensate. It doesn't swing one way and then just come back to the centre and stop, and this same law is also true in life. If things are exceptionally great, they flow easily – you feel wonderful, have loads of energy and life just feels easy. Then, by law, this will be followed by days when everything feels difficult and rubbish for no reason at all. The same tasks that felt easy to do one week can feel like there is a bag of cement attached to them the next! This applies to everything, to all areas of life, from health and relationships to career, money and all others.

Everything flows up and down, so there will always be a corresponding peak for every trough. This is so important to grasp because it can give you a sense of peace, knowing that when things aren't great and the pendulum of life has swung in the direction of the unwanted, where life feels hard, you can rest assured that it's not forever. The Law of Rhythm is at work and so it will swing back to where life feels good again. The way to utilise this law is to accept that when the lows happen, no matter how far down they may pull you, they are temporary. Holding this in mind is such a gift during those times and can help you stay focused on what you want, no matter what.

Working with this law is how you can create balance – by avoiding the super big highs followed by the really big lows. The more balanced you are on the scale, the less swing there will be in either direction. Now, this doesn't mean living a life with no high points; it's about finding a balance through the ups and the downs. Rather than living life at the extremes, from obsessive or overly excited to completely depressed, look for the opposite in each of them to create balance. So when things are really great and you feel like jumping around like an enthusiastic bunny shouting from the rooftops, find calm and peace within that. If you find yourself feeling obsessed by something, seek out other things you can do to steady your attention. This will prevent the pendulum from going so far in one direction and therefore having to swing back in equal measure.

ACTIVATION POINT – *Applying the Law of Rhythm*

When you experience a super high in your life, look for the calm within it. Find moments of peace whilst you enjoy the upside of your experience.

- **Create a list of things that ground you so you have them available to put into practice without having to think about it.**

  This could be something as simple as taking a bath, meditating, walking in nature or doing something positive to help someone who has less than you.

When you experience a moment that is on the lower end of the feel-good scale, it's important to keep focused on your goal, even if it seems impossible to achieve in that moment.

- **Make a list of all the things that are within your control (there may only be a few!).**

  Only work on the things from your list; forget about everything else beyond that, which will usually be outside of your control anyway.

When the pendulum has swung in the direction where you don't feel so good, keep things really simple. Attempting to do too much can very quickly become overwhelming and lead to feeling even worse. Relax knowing that this too shall pass. Ironically, the more accepting you become, the better you will feel and, as a result, the quicker it passes.

Law #6: Law of Cause and Effect

"Every cause has an effect, every effect has its cause, and every action has its reaction."

This law states that there are no accidents in life. Everything that exists within your reality – good and bad – is a consequence of the thoughts and actions that preceded it; nothing happens by chance.

This law is really about taking full responsibility for your life, understanding that wherever you are right now, wherever you have found yourself, is the result of the choices you have made so far. Of course, there will have been times in the past when you had little control over experiences, yet what you always have control over is how you respond to them and how you choose to use those experiences to create what happens in the future.

Think of cause and effect like an equation: the cause equals the effect that follows, or, for every effect that happens, there is something that caused it. We can choose which side of the equation to operate and live our lives from. A life at the cause side is one where you accept that every effect that happens was, is and always will be caused by you. It's taking FULL responsibility for all of your life, which is the only way you can really make changes to it.

This really is not the most appealing way to live. It can be uncomfortable at times but it's also the most empowering!

Life on the effect side of the equation is a life of blame, reasons and excuses about why things aren't the way you want them to be, whether it's because of age, having children, the economy, time, not having a good enough education, the wrong upbringing, the wrong hair colour, being too short, too tall... the list goes on!

This way of living is highly encouraged by society and it keeps people stuck in their problems. Whilst it may appear easier to blame the world and everyone in it for how your life has turned out, it gives your power away and takes your energy with it.

Living life at the effect side of things is the quickest way to have no influence over how it turns out. This is leaving things to fate rather than acknowledging that it's up to you to be in the driving seat of your own life. You have no power when living in effect; you cannot cause any change.

Although it can seem more comfortable at times, relinquishing all responsibility for the way your life is, is actually really hard. Life just happens to these people and they find all the external reasons why things aren't the way they want them to be. The first obstacle that presents itself is a great excuse to give up. If everyone used their circumstances as the reason to not have the life they want, then we would undoubtedly live in a world with little achievement.

Carl Jung, a famous psychiatrist, said:

> *"Until you make the unconscious conscious,*
> *it will direct your life and you will call it fate."*

Making the unconscious conscious is about becoming aware of the patterns you repeat, the thoughts you have, the behaviours you carry out and whether the effect they are producing is what you want. If it isn't, then it's time to make some changes.

This law can also be used as a feedback mechanism. The cause, or the input, creates the effect, or the result. If you're not sure what you've been thinking and how you've been behaving until now, you can reverse engineer what is and isn't working by looking at the results you have, the effects of your current input. Use this information to determine what caused the result. And if you don't like it, work out what needs to change.

The Law of Cause and Effect exists on all four planes of existence: the spiritual, the emotional, the mental and the physical.

On the spiritual plane, cause and effect happens instantly and so it can appear that cause and effect are not separate from each other. On the other planes, we have the concept of time and space and so this creates a time delay between the onset of the cause and the effect that eventually follows. For example, on the physical plane, it's accepted that, over time, eating certain foods or doing certain exercises will affect a person's weight and health.

Food/Exercise (cause) = Weight/Health (effect)

If the effect is unwanted, change the cause and the effect has to change too.

When your desires have a focused intention driving them, they are automatically created on the spiritual plane, and 'as above, so below' means that the physical reality must follow in time; that is, unless you change the input to something that contradicts it.

A life at effect is a life of regret. You only have to imagine yourself taking your last breath with a long list of reasons and excuses as to why it wasn't the life you could've had to know this is true. There is no reason or excuse great enough to not live the life you want!

ACTIVATION POINT – *Applying the Law of Cause and Effect*

To create something new or different, you must first become aware that it exists by making it conscious and then take responsibility for changing it.

Become aware of your thoughts, feelings and behaviours as these are what will cause the effects that follow.

- **Every evening, write down what happened that day that was outside of your control and your response to it.**

   Putting things outside of your control means it's outside of your control to change them.

- **Choose to take responsibility.**

  Acknowledge that you cannot always change the external circumstances or people in them. The only thing you can change is you and that is your responsibility, no one else's.

- **Choose where you would like to make changes and adapt your response next time. Decide what you will do instead that puts you in the driving seat.**

  It is only then that you can make changes. Just pretend you are responsible for EVERYTHING that happens in your life, even if you don't quite believe it yet.

- **Change the word 'can't' to the word 'won't'.**

  This simple shift makes a massive difference. It turns what you do or don't do into a choice, putting you in control.

  It also allows you to forget about the things you're not doing rather than creating a vicious cycle of *"I can't do it,"* shortly followed by *"I should've done it,"* which can then lead to *"I'm such a failure."*

  Instead of going through all the reasons and excuses why you 'can't' do things, accept responsibility that you 'won't' do them – because they are not as important as other things right now and that's okay. It's your choice and that is empowering!

Law #7: Law of Gender

"Gender is in everything; everything has its masculine and feminine principles; gender manifests on all planes."

The Law of Gender is not about gender itself; it's about masculine and feminine energy, both of which are found in everything.

Feminine energy is expressed through intuition, love, care and gentleness; it's emitted from your unconscious mind, where your emotions live. This is true in nature, hence the term 'mother nature'. Feminine energy is the newness of life, being impregnated, quite literally on the physical plane and also with new ideas. It's where creativity is born.

Masculine energy is linear. It's a directed, focused energy where intentions are set and carried out. It's the energy of getting stuff done!

To create the life you desire, it's important to have a balance of the two energies. Many people get stuck in one or the other at different times in their life.

The female is the receiver and the male is the director, a powerful combination!

Let me explain. The feminine part of your mind is where you receive ideas and inspiration, where everything is given birth to. Whilst you need feminine energy for the creation process, the energy itself has no specific aim – it's flowing all over the place. Masculine energy then directs those ideas to bring them into existence through focus and will. In order to maximise the potential of your own mind, you need to have both parts working together.

Be aware that if you don't utilise your own masculine energy, you won't be the one directing your life and if you're not the one doing it, that means someone else is. Those who are mentally strong-willed have a lot of masculine energy and this will influence those who haven't tapped into their own masculine power. This is why many people end up taking on the energy of whoever they are following at that time, whether that's someone speaking on the latest podcast, at an event or training, colleagues, friends and anyone else who has a strong masculine energy. They end up channelling that person's energy rather than learning how to work with their own.

When you allow yourself to let go of what you think about the world, who you are, the structures and belief systems you have taken on, you release the resistance of trying to be, do or have what you think you 'should'.

The clearer and more open you are to being the true version of you, the easier it is to tap into your own source energy to come up with your own ideas. Taking those ideas and writing them down gives you focus so you can channel your masculine power to start making them a reality.

There are standards that people impose upon themselves as a measure of their own success – the relationship, the education, the house, the car, the holidays – and hey, if those are the things you desire, great. That's okay! The point is that throughout the whole of the country you live in, even the world, there really is no way that almost every single person wants exactly the same things, yet so many of us strive for the same results.

If nothing more, I encourage you to take the time to be really honest with yourself about whether you are being true to yourself or allowing the masculine energy outside of you to influence your direction. If you're going to spend time working on intentionally creating your life, it may as well be one that you want, rather than what others say you should have.

ACTIVATION POINT – *Applying the Law of Gender*

Time to be honest with yourself!

- **If comparison didn't exist and no one would ever know what you did or didn't do, had, or didn't have, what is it you truly desire?**

  Allow yourself to answer this fully by putting pen to paper and answer as though no one is watching, so you can be you.

- **Notice where you spend the majority of your time. Are you always taking action and pushing, using your will? Or do you go with the flow, letting your inspiration guide you with very little action?**

  Of course, you may be doing a mixture of both, but you will usually find that you favour one over the other.

  Consider where you may benefit from balancing your energy to utilise both masculine and feminine.

- **Allow time for creativity, self-care and inspiration, embracing your feminine energy whilst also using your masculine energy for direction and focus when taking action.**

  Remember, you have both masculine and feminine energy within you and working together with both in partnership gives you access to the divine feminine of birth and creation of ideas, as well as the masculine to bring those ideas into the physical world.

So that's just a brief overview of the universal laws and how they relate to your world. I invite and encourage you to keep them in mind at all times. Refer back to them to check if there is a law you haven't been practising or haven't considered. Use them as a guide whilst, at the same time, not being at the effect of them. The laws aren't to blame for the situations you find yourself in, so using them as the reason why you haven't got the life you want would be putting responsibility outside of you, and ignoring the Law of Cause and Effect.

The laws are always at play, just like the Law of Gravity, so working with them is one way to begin to become the creator of your reality.

Chapter 3
The Rowing Boat and the Submarine

"In a very real sense we have two minds,
one that thinks and one that feels."
Daniel Goleman

Many years ago, I worked with a coaching client who couldn't understand why she ruined the good things in her life. For confidentiality reasons, we'll call her Kelly. Kelly had a pattern of sabotaging anything positive.

I remember one of our sessions where she told me about the previous Friday evening when she'd felt compelled to create an issue where there really wasn't one.

"I was curled up on the couch last Friday evening, watching the TV with a hot chocolate and my favourite biscuits, which I had been

looking forward to all week! I've spent the last three months following a healthy eating plan ready for my holiday but every Friday evening I allow myself my little piece of heaven.

It was 7.38pm and my partner, Darren, was late home from playing squash. It's been his thing for years and every Friday evening he plays in a local tournament. When we moved in together, he offered to play less so we could spend more time with each other, but I could see how passionate he was about it, so I encouraged him to continue playing. His passion is one of the things I love most about him.

He said he'd be home for 7.30pm, but I know some weeks it does run over slightly, if the game goes on longer than usual or if there's traffic on the way home, but he's usually no later than 7.45pm.

I knew this, but last week I found myself feeling irritated. Every 30 seconds I was glancing at the clock. I could feel my foot tapping but couldn't seem to stop it and I struggled to pay attention to whatever was on the TV.

We're part-way through a TV series that we watch together and I usually wait for him to get home to watch it but I had already made my hot chocolate and I wanted to drink it with the series whilst it was still hot. With every passing minute, I could feel myself becoming more and more annoyed!

This really bothered me because Darren is the most kind and considerate partner and I was the one who encouraged him to carry on playing squash. I've always considered myself to be a rational person and so couldn't understand why I was feeling so much emotion over something so minor.

I knew Darren would probably walk through the door any minute as he always did. I know he loves me; he shows me all the time and I knew he would be keen to get home, and so there really wasn't any issue with him being a few minutes late. I had no logical reason to feel the way I did but even with all the evidence stacked up in front of me, I was not feeling rational.

The thing that worries me the most was that I might not be good at hiding the way I feel and I could end up driving away the man I love. I could sabotage a brilliant relationship that I really want to keep. Whilst that evening itself is such a seemingly small thing, I've felt this way before over other things and I'm scared it could lead to much bigger consequences.

I don't want to feel this way but I do and I don't know why or what to do about it."

Kelly's story has so many similarities with other stories and problems that clients have come to me with over the years. She wants to feel okay but the more she resisted her emotions and argued with them, the harder they seemed to fight back.

It probably comes as no surprise that rational thinking goes out of the window when it comes to emotions. You can try as much as you like but when emotions are high, thinking like a reasoned person doesn't happen easily, if at all.

It can sometimes feel as though your inner world has many different characters or, to put it another way, it can feel like you have a split personality going on. You're thinking one thing but the way you feel is in total opposition and, whilst you may know that, rationally, the way you feel doesn't make any sense at all – you still feel it.

Take a breath! You can be rest assured that you are completely sane… even though I know first-hand that the evidence can make you feel otherwise at times.

We're going to touch on the mechanics of your internal world and how it operates, which is the key to begin taking control of your external world.

Conscious and Unconscious

To explain the phenomena that are us mere mortals, I'd like to introduce you to your mind or, to be more accurate, your two minds!

I want to be clear that you do only have one physical mind, but for the purpose of explaining how the mind operates, imagine having two minds living in the same space. Both minds have distinctive roles and those roles have very different functions, but both are equally important. Having an insight into the difference between them can help you identify which mind to work with to make positive changes and deal with issues when they present themselves along the way.

Say hello to your conscious mind and your unconscious mind.

You may well have heard of them both many times before but I'm going to go through an overview of their roles and functions in a way that will bring them to life, so you can become more familiar with them as you progress through the following chapters.

The following information is based on the study of neuro linguistic programming (NLP), developed in the 1970s by Richard Bandler and John Grinder. NLP is the study of how our brains process and interpret information, which results in the thoughts we think and our feelings, which leads to our behaviour and, ultimately, the results we get.

To give you a metaphor that will assist you with this, I want you to think of your conscious mind as a rowing boat, floating on the surface of a large ocean, and your unconscious mind as a submarine under the water, with the two of them tied together by a piece of rope.

When a person wants to change direction in life, to metaphorically head towards a new destination, they will usually put all their effort into turning the rowing boat around by rowing harder and faster. The problem with this is that the submarine is still pulling in the original direction, the opposite way. If I had to place a bet on whether the rowing boat or the submarine would win, I know where I would put my money! Fighting a submarine would be hard work for anyone.

The submarine, your unconscious mind, is responsible for and drives approximately a whopping 95% of what you do or don't do. That leaves the remaining 5%, which is the rowing boat – your conscious mind. Your conscious mind is only responsible for 5% for your thoughts, feelings and the action you take.

When you think of it like that, I'm sure you can appreciate why working hard in your rowing boat can feel like you're doing a lot but getting nowhere fast.

Before we dive underwater to the submarine, where you'll get to know your unconscious mind, let's get acquainted with what's on top of the water, the rowing boat – your conscious mind and the role it plays.

Your Conscious Mind

According to *Oxford Living Dictionaries*, the word 'consciousness' by definition means *"the state of being aware of and responsive to one's surroundings"*, or, *"a person's awareness or perception of something"*. Consciousness is basically everything you are conscious or aware of.

Your conscious mind is located in the left hemisphere of your brain; it's your logical thinking brain where you rationalise and make sense of things. This is the mind that Kelly was using to try to convince herself that she was being silly, because the way she felt made no logical sense.

As you go about your everyday, you are consciously aware of your surroundings and your experience within them. You take your world – all the things you can see, hear, feel, taste and smell – in through your five senses. Every second of every single day, everything that happens outside of you, literally everything, is being taken in through your senses, yet so much of that information is outside of your conscious awareness.

Follow along with this exercise for a moment so you can experience it for yourself:

Pause for a moment and take in just a few of the things you can see, hear, feel, smell and taste. How many things do you notice?

Now spread your awareness even further, and become aware of the sounds in the distance, the feeling of your left small toe, the temperature of your skin, the feeling of the ground beneath you, your breath as it goes in and out, your right kneecap, the people passing by, the noise of the cars, the smell of next-door's food cooking or their dog barking, all the things that are the colour brown around you.

These things have always been there but you probably hadn't noticed them. In your reality they didn't exist, because you were busy focusing on other things. That was until they were brought to your attention, into your conscious awareness. Now, of course, our physical bodies go everywhere we do, so on some level we know they're always there, but the same principle applies to the things happening outside of you too. The things you are aware of in any moment are the things you are focusing on. As soon as you change your focus to something new, you are no longer thinking about those other things anymore.

The power of focus is what allows you to really home in on what you are doing, dismissing everything else that is going on around you. Your conscious mind by its very nature has a very narrow, laser-like focus because of its capacity to only hold a small amount of information at any one time. Even when its focus is only held on a particular thing for a split second, it will be solely on it in that single moment. When you train yourself to focus your attention in the right direction – in other words, on what you want – your conscious mind can be hugely powerful in helping you create your desired reality, if you use it in the way it was intended.

"What consumes your mind controls your life."
Anonymous

When your awareness is focused quite literally on one thing, you can find yourself consciously consumed by it. The tunnel-like vision that it provides you with, if you choose to tap into it, is the very thing that makes some people successful in ways that many only dream of. It is the ability to block out any other conflicting information and create a path of certainty inside oneself.

Of course, as with anything in life, there is a flip side to the coin: focus can also be the very reason for things not going well for many people. When your focus is directed towards something unwanted, it can feel all-consuming and with consequences that may not be so favourable.

Activating your RAS on purpose is all about changing the things you are consciously aware of, and to do that we have to go a little deeper first.

Let's say hello to your unconscious mind!

Your Unconscious Mind

The definition of 'unconscious' according to *Oxford Languages* is *"not awake and aware of and responding to one's environment"* or *"done or existing without one realising"*. The unconscious are the things we're not conscious or aware of. Whilst the first definition could relate to being physically unconscious, there is certainly a metaphor within it. When we wake up that part of the brain, we are able to see the endless possibilities that are right in front of us; we activate our RAS.

Your unconscious mind, which is located in the right hemisphere of the brain, is the powerhouse that drives you, your thoughts, feelings and behaviours. It's where all the information happening outside of you is received and processed, even the bits you're not consciously aware of.

The great thing about your unconscious mind is that it runs on autopilot, so you don't actually have to think about it; it just ticks along doing its jobs!

The jobs it has are really important and there are a number of them to do. I'm going to take you through just a few of them so you can begin to grasp how they contribute to the creation of your reality.

I feel for you

Let's talk emotions – the good, the bad and the ugly! Your emotions are not something you pick and choose as you go through your day; they just happen, and most people have little control over them. Kelly knew the way she felt about Darren getting home slightly late was irrational and made no sense at all, yet that's how she felt. This is because emotions happen automatically – they are an unconscious process. Arguing them away with critical thinking and analysis of why you shouldn't feel them doesn't work. You can give yourself a break if the way you're feeling doesn't seem logical. Emotions are not logical!

You are responsive by nature and whilst you can consciously choose how you want to feel and may use many of the fantastic techniques to help you do that (such as embodying and imagining the feeling you desire, affirmations, breathing deeply and smiling), when you go about your day, you feel the wide variety of emotions that are available to us as humans. Everything, from happiness, sadness and anger to guilt, fear and every other emotion in between, and the feelings you experience happen unconsciously in response to internal and external factors.

It's all in the bag

All of your memories – the positive and the negative, every single one that has ever happened to you – are stored in your unconscious mind, even those things you can't remember consciously, no matter how hard you try. If you were to try to remember what a particular person said to you at your seventh birthday party just before you opened your presents, that may not be so easy to do, yet even though you can't remember it, the memory is stored away in your unconscious mind. This is the reason why you may find yourself randomly remembering things, events and conversations that took place years ago that you'd completely forgotten about. The memory was always there; it was just tucked away in your unconscious until that moment.

If you've had the privilege of being on this planet for a number of years, the chances are you have more than a couple of memories stored away from different times in your life. From childhood to leaving school, starting your first job, maybe getting married, having a family and beyond. In order for you to mentally make sense of all those memories and distinguish the difference between something that happened five years ago, 10 years ago, yesterday, today, or even something you imagine happening in the future, your memories are organised within your mental timeline – an internal filing system that is totally unique to you. Your unconscious filing system is where all the files of your life are recorded, stored and ordered in a sequence, so you can differentiate the time at which they took place.

It's important to note that not all memories are created equal and this is where your unconscious mind is extremely clever! There are those memories that, when you think about them, bring you complete joy. Then there are those you might prefer to forget about entirely.

Some memories will have a lot of emotion attached to them and at the time those emotional events occurred, you may not have been in the position to deal with them, mentally, emotionally or even physically. Here's where the clever part comes in. Your unconscious mind takes those memories and puts them in a metaphorical box, hidden out of sight with a lid on it. This allows you to go about your everyday life without having to think about and deal with any memories that are too painful in that moment. Your unconscious mind's job is to protect you and so it will keep those memories repressed until you are in a position to be able to deal with them.

The very nature of life means that you will inevitably have experiences you could call 'character building'. Events that result in you becoming stronger and more resourceful; what doesn't kill you makes you stronger, right?!

When you deal with and overcome hard times, you build mental and emotional strength and you're then in a position where you feel equipped to handle those things in the future, things you wouldn't have been able to in the past. We've all had an experience that, at the time, felt impossible to overcome but now you would find much easier.

Your unconscious mind has all of your memories logged and stored away for a later date, ready for when you are able to deal with them. It recognises when the strength needed to work through them is available, when you have the internal resources to cope. It's only then that those repressed memories will be presented to your conscious mind; you will become aware of them so that you can finally resolve them and let go of any associated negative emotions.

The time those memories are presented is, more often than not, when things are going great and you find yourself thinking about something from the past, a time in your life or an event that wasn't as good. Although it may seem to appear completely out of the blue, it is because you are ready for it – you are able to deal with it! Your unconscious mind will only ever give you as much as you can handle, so see this as a good sign that you must have grown. It's an opportunity to learn from the past, let it go and move forward even stronger.

Like anything in life, the first time we do anything, it can feel impossible, from playing an instrument, lifting weights in the gym, asking someone out or talking in public to name a few. When you do it, your mind proves that you're okay and you can handle it; you build mental resilience. The more resilient you are, the more your mind will give you to work through. This offers a whole new perspective: what could be seen as something negative can be reframed as something really positive.

Just relax. I've got it

You may never have given this much thought before now but your body is so clever; it just does its thing and works, hence why you don't have to think about it. You can rest easy knowing that, unless there is a problem, your heart will just keep on pumping and you will keep breathing every single second of the day.

How wonderful that your body runs itself. You have your unconscious mind to thank for that! It takes care of the running of your body for you so you don't have to think about it. In fact, one of its most important functions is to run and preserve your body.

Your unconscious mind also knows what health is and how it feels when the body is running exactly as it should. This is why you know when you're feeling unwell – even if you're not sure exactly what is wrong, you know that something is. You have the blueprint of perfect health stored within you and when it's not present, there will be a signal that tells you so. This could come in the form of a niggle that something isn't quite right or that you need to slow down. Maybe something feels off and the voice in your head keeps prodding you to listen. We've all experienced those times when we chose to ignore the subtle signs until they got bigger and louder and we discovered that we were right! The number of times I've told myself I need some rest and I kept going anyway – that is, until my body made me rest. Whether it's through illness or injury, eventually your body will give in. Those signs, signals and whispers are your unconscious mind, so practise listening to them and trust yourself rather than waiting to prove yourself right.

Your wish is my command

There is one role of the unconscious mind that I know you are just going to love. Unlike many people, it relishes being told what to do. Finally, you have someone you can just give instructions to and they will be welcomed with open arms. Hooray! And the best news is, that someone is you.

But like anything in life, instructions can sometimes be misunderstood, so there are a couple of keys to make sure the instructions you give yourself are received by your unconscious mind in the way you intend.

The first key is that the instructions need to be super simple and very clear. Sounds obvious, yet it can easily become anything but straightforward.

Being complicated doesn't mean something is better. It doesn't necessarily add depth or intelligence; it can just complicate things, and your unconscious mind does not respond well to confusion. The best way to really get to grips with this is to think of your unconscious mind as though it is a young child, so make your instructions as easy to follow as possible.

Imagine you're in the supermarket with a young child and you ask them to go get some tomatoes. That's a pretty simple instruction to follow but it's not a very clear one. There are so many varieties of tomatoes to choose from, everything from fresh tomatoes, including cherry, plum, salad and beef, not to mention the tinned options of chopped, plum, with added herbs... A young child is likely to not know where to begin and so will most likely pick the one they see first. You may well be hoping for one type of tomato and end up with something completely different to what you actually wanted. This is not only true when buying tomatoes; it's also true in all areas of life.

Being clear also means being consistent, because a lack of consistency causes confusion.

The messages we give out are often mixed. Imagine that one day you told a young child that they are great, that they can do anything they put their mind to and they should go for their dreams. Then, the next day you told them they are worthless and should stay at home and hide under a pillow before someone sees them and realises how rubbish they are. I dare say you wouldn't dream of it! Yet that is exactly how so many people treat their unconscious mind, which is ultimately how they are treating themselves. Having an aspiration dream they are excited about but then telling themselves not to go for it because they're not capable of achieving it. Feeling good one day and then beating themselves up the next. Taking steps towards something and then completely backing off again.

The unconscious mind takes on all instructions and even if they contradict each other, it will follow them all. This is not only confusing to you but also others outside of you. It appears to the outside world as being flaky and inconsistent, like someone who is always changing their mind, feeling up and down and never sticking to something or seeing it through. This is something I used to do every hour, never mind every day, and I imagine you have experienced this in yourself at one time or another in your life.

Always give very clear and consistent instructions to your unconscious mind, even if you don't quite believe them to be true yet. Just like a young child learning to ride a bike, the more you do this, the easier it will become. Be kind to yourself like you would be to a young child, too. If you find yourself being anything less than compassionate, stop and consider if you would ever treat another person, let alone a child, in the same way. You were a young child once and whilst you have grown up, that child still exists within you. The kinder you are to yourself, the more love you will have available for others.

The next key to making sure your instructions are received correctly is to ensure they are focused on what you want rather than what you don't want.

This is really important. It's super simple when you know it and although it's such a common mistake, it can be easily rectified. The reason this is critical to creating your reality is because the unconscious mind doesn't process negatives. I'm not talking about whether you're trying to be positive or not; this is referring to words that negate: words such as don't (do not), won't (will not), can't (cannot). The negating word doesn't register with the unconscious mind so when you instruct yourself NOT to do something, all your unconscious mind will hear is the instruction itself.

Let me demonstrate how this works. If I asked you to NOT think of a red apple, I can guarantee you would think of a red apple. This is because your unconscious mind processes what to think about in order to NOT think about it, and your attention is then on that very thing.

This happens a lot when people are pursuing goals, and it's something I used to do in the past. Many people find it easy to tell you exactly what they don't want and spend their time and energy in an effort to avoid those very things. Affirming over and over again about how…

"I don't want to be in debt" – my focus is on debt and how much I have

"I'm going to stop eating chocolate" – all I can think about is chocolate

"I'm not going to hit the snooze when my alarm goes off" – snooze, snooze, snooze

"I won't be in the job I hate by this time next year" – oh no!

The list goes one!

If you're constantly telling yourself what not to do, that is the message your unconscious mind will process. It will be the movie that plays out in your mind, the things you think about and focus on. Aside from the fact that it won't lead you to manifesting the life you dream of anytime soon, it's not the best movie to watch over and over again. You'd never choose to watch a film that kept repeating a scene you didn't want to see, a movie that doesn't feel good, yet this is how people live their lives.

You are literally giving your mind instructions all day every day through the things you choose to focus on. So, always focus on and say what it is you do want rather than what you don't want.

If you don't know what you want right now, that's okay. The starting point to knowing what you want is to know what you don't want, so you're already on your way! You can begin flipping the direction of your thoughts by considering what the opposite of the unwanted things are as you continue working your way through this book.

When the instructions you give your unconscious mind are clear, simple and focused on the outcome you desire, you activate your RAS to find ways to fulfil those instructions. It is on high alert whenever an opportunity that matches it is within reach.

It's all about me

This is a really interesting one. If you've ever found yourself saying anything less than nice things about someone or something, then this is very important to know: your unconscious mind takes everything personally. It doesn't know that your thoughts or words are being directed at someone outside of you and so it takes it as an instruction or suggestion to itself. It's very literal! This is where the saying *"when you point one finger, there are three fingers pointing back at you"* comes from. If I were to give you any advice, it would be to say nice things about others and really mean it. This may take a little practice when you first begin but when you truly know that you really can be, do and have whatever you want in your own life, it makes sense to wish everyone else well in theirs too.

If you ever find yourself experiencing any kind of negative emotions about the success of others, it's okay. We've all been there! Watching someone else having the very experience or achieving the thing that you want but haven't yet can certainly bring those emotions to the surface. The truth is that those emotions have absolutely nothing to do with the person or thing that prompted their appearance. It's really about you and the beliefs about lack and scarcity that you hold about it being possible in your life. That lack could be in the form of a belief you hold that limits, or emotions that prevent, you from also achieving it.

Think about it like this. If someone across the road bought themselves a new fancy lawnmower, the way you feel about that neighbour and their lawnmower is nothing to do with them. If you wholeheartedly believe that you, too, can have a lawnmower, or you don't really care about lawnmowers at all, then you'll probably feel nothing about their lawnmower either. You may even not realise they have one! Whereas, if you didn't believe you could have the same lawnmower, maybe you couldn't afford it in that moment or you didn't think you'd be capable of using it, then you may well have negative feelings about the neighbour and their lawnmower.

Usually, people will direct the lack they feel towards their neighbour, calling them names like 'show-off', 'shallow', 'all about the money', 'compensating for lack in other areas' – all without cause or any real evidence to support such accusations.

When those emotions come out to say hello, it's a great opportunity to turn them back onto yourself and ask, what is really going on? The lawnmower itself, or any other garden machinery, object or occurrence in life is irrelevant; it's purely a representation of you and what's going on internally. How you perceive others is actually extremely useful information about you and what you believe to be possible. It's the best feedback we could ever wish for! Rather than pointing the finger at others and noticing what you don't like about them, consider for a moment why that might be. What is it within you that needs addressing that is being reflected back at you?

It's also worth keeping in mind that your own unconscious mind will take any negative thoughts directed at someone else personally as a suggestion to yourself, which will programme your own mind to think that way. Asking for something you desire and then resenting the presence of it will only push it away further.

This concept works both ways, so there is the opposite side too. Any time you notice the good things outside of you, those things are also true about you. For you to notice them in others, they must be within you in the first place. Recognising them is an opportunity to reinforce what your inner being already knows. Even if there are some things you aren't fully on board with being true just yet, just accepting that it's possible on some level is a step in the right direction.

If you have been anything less than positive about others up to now, which we all have at some point, give yourself a break. Everyone is doing the best they can with what is available to them in that moment. Hindsight is a wonderful thing and it's easy to look back at how you would do things differently given the same experiences. Let's face it, if you hadn't had those times where you may have behaved in a way that makes you shudder when you think of them today, then you wouldn't have had the opportunity to learn from them and be who you are now. The power you have to change things is always now!

Willpower is not enough

Willpower. Even the word itself feels like hard work and if you've ever tried making changes through willpower alone, then you'll know that it is! Willpower often requires going against ingrained habits, thoughts and behaviours.

The problem with that is the habits and behaviours we have are not what we consciously choose; they are formed in the unconscious part of our minds. No matter how many times you tell yourself you will stop biting your nails or heading straight to the fridge the minute you walk through the kitchen door, your unconscious autopilot kicks in and it's usually only after the event that you realise you've done it. Even if you consciously manage to intervene in the moment and stop yourself, it's not easy to do and uses a lot of energy to resist, because those programmes run automatically. Your mind is continuing to think about or do the thing you don't want, even if your body isn't. So even though the chocolate may have been left in the cupboard, your mind is there with it!

To relate this to the rowing boat and the submarine, imagine the rowing boat (your conscious mind) has been heading in a certain direction for a while, to a destination called Boredomville. I'm sure you can guess by the name that it's not the most exciting place in the world!

The rowing boat is floating along every day, sailing closer towards a destination that you don't really want to go. Boredomville is the place where you work in a job you don't like, stay in an unhappy relationship, eat junk food, feel tired, wish the weeks away and, generally, life isn't what you know it could be. Although you may not like it there, the actions you take continue to lead to Boredomville.

One day you decide it's time to make changes. Boredomville isn't cutting it anymore. You've had enough and realise it's time to make some positive changes. You plan to form new ways of thinking, new ways of behaving and you're going to be upbeat about it. You feel determined and motivated and so you take action to do just that. You begin turning the boat around. You use your oars to point yourself towards a new destination, a place called Fulfillmentville, where life is, you've guessed it, fulfilling. It's a place where you do work that you love, surrounded by people you enjoy spending time with; you feel energised, healthy and exhilarated by life.

The changes needed to get there are happening. You're going to the gym, eating healthily, reading books, meditating, setting up a new business, looking for new friends who are also heading to Fulfillmentville. You put the work in, pushing your oars hard from inside the rowing boat, making a conscious effort, thinking about your choices and working hard. Bit by bit, you begin heading towards your new life.

It sounds good, doesn't it? But there is an issue!

You're pushing really hard, tirelessly working from inside the rowing boat but what you haven't considered is that the rowing boat is still tied to the submarine, and the submarine hasn't been reprogrammed. It's still set to head towards Boredomville and so it carries on its usual route. No matter how forcefully you row, you're fighting against the big submarine under the water, pulling you in the opposite direction. Determination will only keep you going for a while and it soon becomes really tiring. The submarine is just too big and eventually, the pull from it feels so strong that you run out of steam and stop fighting it.

When you think about making changes in this way, it's no wonder so many people give up when willpower is the only thing that got them started in the first place.

Our unconscious programmes make carrying out patterns of behaviours easy to do with very little cognitive effort, which is super useful; it means you don't have to think about every little thing you do day to day, making life easier. You are programmed to brush your teeth, drive a car, cross your arms, all without thinking. (Try crossing your arms the opposite way to what you usually would and notice how much you have to consciously think about where they go!) Imagine having to think about absolutely everything you do. There wouldn't be time for anything else but the basics, if you even made it that far!

These programmes are also amazing when they are programmed to take you towards Fulfillmentville, to the life you want to create. They are not so helpful when they are programmed in the opposite direction of your dreams and goals. This leads to so many people giving up when they don't see the instant reward for the effort they put in. Change through willpower and conscious effort is flipping tough and, because it takes a lot of brain power, when results don't happen quickly or easily, it feels too hard to carry on. Giving up becomes very appealing and people will reason with themselves as to why it's a good idea to do so.

I spent many days telling myself that life is short and it's important to enjoy it, so I should have that extra dessert or glass of wine;

I shouldn't wear myself out working too hard, getting up early every day – I could die tomorrow! Whilst you could say this is all true, I was looking for excuses to not make progress, because it felt too much like work, like a battle, and no one wants to go to war, especially with themselves. My conscious mind would look for the logic behind giving up but the problem was that my unconscious mind knew the truth. It knew I wanted all the things I dreamt about; I just didn't have the beliefs and drive to support myself in getting them.

All of that being said, willpower can win out over a period of time, although it's less common as most give up before reaching the threshold needed to make it stick. There are varying studies that show it takes at least 21 to 66 consistent days to form a new habit using conscious willpower alone. The 21-day theory was first discovered when Dr Maxwell Maltz, a plastic surgeon in the 1950s, performed operations. He noticed a trend of people taking 21 days to adapt to new situations in their life. This included everything from having a nose reconstruction to a limb being amputated. After 21 days, he found that people had adjusted to the change. New research from Phillippa Lally has since found that the average time it takes to perform a new behaviour on autopilot is 66 days. Either way, the message here is that continuous repetition is key.

When you make changes consciously, the rowing boat is attempting to pull the submarine along with it. Bit by bit, day by day, slowing the submarine down until it is able to be redirected. This absolutely can be done but, just like a rowing boat pulling a submarine, it's not easy. When you consciously tell yourself you are going to do something and your unconscious mind, your thoughts, beliefs, self-talk and emotions don't match what you are saying, it feels as tough as pulling a submarine in the opposite direction of the path it's programmed to follow.

The unconscious mind has been programmed to head in a certain direction and it becomes familiar with the route; it's known, it feels safe and so it's easy to revert back to the comfortable, most trodden pathway, even if it's not the pathway that leads to where you want to go.

Changes through willpower can be done and one of the biggest keys to making them stick is consistency. To change the submarine's direction, it needs to be pulled a little bit, every single day for 21–66 days in a row. Consistently really does mean consistently!

When you begin your new way of being, if at any point during the 21–66 consistent days you happen to slip up and revert to old behaviours and habits, the submarine returns to its original track, heading back towards Boredomville. Carrying out the unwanted behaviours before the submarine has fully reprogrammed its route will cause the submarine to resume its path. If that happens, the 21–66 days resets and you have to begin again from Day One, pulling the submarine a small bit at a time!

To put this into real-life context, if someone gives up smoking and doesn't have a cigarette for 15 days in a row, the submarine will begin to slow down, ready to re-route itself in the direction of being a non-smoker. The habits are starting to form and become the new way of thinking and behaving. If, on Day 16, that person has a cigarette, the submarine reverts back to the original unwanted path. It resumes the thought patterns, beliefs and drivers that support them in being a smoker and so they feel compelled to behave like one, i.e. to smoke. The submarine is back on its original route; it just took a slight detour for a while.

There is something positive that happens in the process – all is not lost!

By this point, the submarine has spent some time pointing towards and treading the new path, even if just for a short period of time, so it has a reference point for the new route and there was a little momentum created on the way. This makes it much easier to go that way again because the mental muscle that shows you that it can be done is already in place, which makes picking up those metaphorical weights easier to do a second time around.

If you do manage to keep on track consistently for 21–66 days, having practised the new way of doing things without reverting back to old habits, the submarine is then reprogrammed to head for the desired destination, to Fulfillmentville. It gets to the point where it's easier to keep going, to continue carrying out the new way of being, than it is to go back to the original route. It becomes the new automatic programme and, most importantly, the rowing boat and the submarine are going to the same place, cheering each other on. This is alignment!

Consciously pursuing something you haven't done before, whether it's learning a new skill or behaving differently, will usually start out with you being completely unaware of how to do it or it feeling unnatural to you. This is really hard mental work; there can be a lot of frustration and confusion, and giving up can seem like the easier option. But if you keep going, one day at a time, there comes a point where it suddenly seems to slot into place and you can just do it – it happens easily without thought.

To help make changes you are more likely to stick to, choose to focus your attention on completing just one day at a time. Doing so takes it from what can feel like a mammoth task to just accomplishing something for 16 hours, since you'll probably be asleep for the other eight. At the end of every 24 hours, you will feel like you have achieved a mini goal, which will spur you on to do more. It will then feel less about willpower and more about carrying on with the good work you have already done.

I remember when I decided to start learning to play the guitar, I kept forgetting to even practise. I had to put it on my phone calendar with an alert to remind me, otherwise I unconsciously carried out my usual activities and it was only at the end of the day that I remembered I'd forgotten.

The first time I picked up a guitar, I felt like I was holding an alien and it sounded like it was out of tune. After a few months of consistently practising (thanks to my alert reminding me to), even though it was hard and my hands physically ached at times, I could suddenly play a few chords without having to think about what I was doing and it sounded like a real song! Picking up my guitar in the evening became something I just did without thinking. This same principle applies to change across the board.

The point at which things begin flowing is when the programming in your submarine has changed – you're on track and the route to Fulfillmentville is now the default direction. That doesn't mean there is no more effort required on your part; it's just that the effort no longer feels like your mind is in opposition and using any energy you have to fight it. Your energy can then be utilised to do the work necessary to achieve what you want. Amazing!

Having a purpose, a reason for making the change, is such a huge motivator too. If there is no reason for doing it, then even the most disciplined would struggle to carry on. We'll talk more about this in later chapters.

Now, I should mention here something that can happen after your unconscious mind has been reprogrammed. It's totally normal for your conscious mind to question things. Being the critical thinker that it is, you may find yourself analysing those changes to convince yourself that it's actually happened. For such a long time the submarine has been heading towards Boredomville... and then it's not, and that can be a little disconcerting. It may take a little time for your conscious mind, sat in the rowing boat, to be certain that the change has happened, that the submarine has really altered its course. If you find yourself feeling sceptical, you now know why and you can just let your conscious mind catch up and be convinced the change has taken place in its own time.

Programming itself is neither good nor bad; it's both wonderful and not so wonderful at the same time. Carrying out the majority of what we do without any brain power allows us to focus on the things that matter to us and require our energy at that time. We are able to carry out the daily tasks without any thought. The first time you learnt how to tie your shoelaces probably felt like an impossible task that you would never achieve, until one day you did. You kept practising and eventually your unconscious mind took over. The programme for how to tie your shoelaces became automatic – you can now do it without consciously thinking about it and this is true of many of the things we do. Programming is hugely beneficial in our lives. This programming also means that much of what we do without thought, even when it isn't serving us, is completely out of our awareness. We just do it and even if we know it's not what we want, it feels easier.

Many of the things we want to stop or start doing, we know about, but not always. So often the things we do that sabotage our success are completely outside of our awareness – we are oblivious to them because we do them on autopilot. Bringing those unconscious patterns into conscious awareness is the first step in changing them. You have to know what it is that needs changing for you to be able to do it.

ACTIVATION POINT – Becoming Aware

At the end of each day, note down the following:

- **What habits, behaviours and thoughts did I carry out that aren't serving me?**

- **What did I do that is keeping me on the path I no longer want to be on?**

- **What did I do that stopped me from heading towards the life I desire?**

- **What didn't I do that would help me move towards the life I desire?**

- **What can I do instead?**

Once you have identified the patterns you're running that are no longer serving you, there are ways you can make changes very quickly at the unconscious level, which will turn the submarine towards Fulfillmentville. If a habit or behaviour is created in the unconscious mind, then it makes sense that changing it also takes place in the unconscious mind. Where it's created is also where it is re-created into something new.

Understanding how lasting change is created is a crucial part of knowing how to make it. You can then begin piecing together the picture of you in relation to what's materialising in your life. The world that you see outside of you, what you are conscious of, all begins and is based on the reality that you hold in your unconscious mind. As within, so without. NLP is the user manual for your mind and the gateway to creating quick and lasting change.

Chapter 4
The Gatekeeper of Your Mind

*The important things will always
make themselves known.*

What is reality? Well, if you were to ask five different people, you would get five different answers, which really makes the point that reality is what you perceive it to be in the moment that you observe it. It's an ever-changing thing and no two people in the entire world ever have, or ever will, experience reality in the exact same way.

Reality is everything that is happening in your awareness at any point in time. Wherever you place your focus in any moment is the only thing that is actually happening in your world right then. Remember, most of the things surrounding you, you won't even notice; your conscious mind just won't process them. You are oblivious to them until you focus on them. Does that mean they weren't there before you fixed your attention on them? Of course they were!

Everything that is happening outside of you, everything you are experiencing, every second of every day, is being taken in through your five senses: what you can see, hear, feel, smell, taste. When I say everything, I mean *everything*! Studies in NLP show that we receive approximately 11 million bits of information per second. To give you an idea of just how much that is, imagine 11 million jellybeans or 11 million people in a stadium bombarding your senses every second of every day. Even if you like jellybeans, that's a lot to process. It's jellybean overload!

It's probably no surprise that your brain isn't able to deal with that amount of information at the rate it's coming in, not consciously anyway. Think about it. If you had 11 million jellybeans coming at you in one go, how could you possibly take in all of the different sizes, the different colours, the tastes, the smells, the sheer number of them? The same thing goes for real life: how could you be aware of every detail that is happening outside of you? The simple answer is, you can't. And the truth is you probably wouldn't want to be. The amount of information your conscious mind can focus on and handle at any one time is limited. It's not physically possible to consciously process 11 million bits at any one time. Because of this, there is a massive number of things happening that are completely beyond your awareness.

The fact that most of what is going on around us all day every day is outside of our awareness is a good thing, otherwise we'd have a meltdown – our minds would go into overdrive. It would be like opening up every program on your computer all at once: there would be too much to handle and it would crash!

You can rest easy knowing that even if your reality isn't how you want it yet, your mind is keeping you sane; it's protecting you. It's one of the reasons you have two minds!

There are many practices that help you change your focus and therefore your reality, but I used to wonder what influenced our focus and our perception of reality in the first place. Who decided which of the 11 million jellybeans or bits of information made their way through the conscious mind and which bits stayed unconscious? When you can get to grips with where that comes from, you begin to understand how to change it and open up your mind to possibilities that had previously gone unnoticed.

Say hello again to your reticular activating system! The gatekeeper to your reality. It's time to take a dive into the mechanics of how your RAS decides what is getting in and what is staying out.

The Mental Security Guard

Your name's not down; you're not coming in!

Imagine, for a moment, a gatekeeper stood outside a building, with a list of what can come in and what cannot, and the rule is that if it's not on the list, then it's not getting through the gate!

This is how your RAS works. It's the gatekeeper of your mind, filtering out anything that isn't on the list and only the things that are will be let through the door. It's only the things on the list, the ones that do get inside, that you then become aware of – they have been allowed into your conscious mind. The rest stay outside the door in your unconscious mind. All of those things left outside are still there. They still exist; you are just oblivious to them.

This begs the question, how does something make its way onto the list?

Years ago, I would take the same route to work every day of the week. I knew the journey like the back of my hand and paid very little attention to my surroundings because I'd seen them hundreds of times before. Then, one day I was chatting with my mum, who is a reiki master amongst other things and loves her crystals. She told me she had been reading about a particular crystal that had all sorts of healing properties and she really wanted one. Being a big believer in energy, she wasn't keen on ordering it online as you never quite know what you'll end up with or be sure about the quality of the crystal, so she was keen to find one that was ethically sourced and genuine.

It was around November time; Christmas was approaching and I was yet to buy presents. In fact, I hadn't even thought about what to get everyone, so I was pleased she had made it easy for me. The crystal was added to my Christmas gift list. A day or so later I was doing my usual drive to work when I noticed a shop tucked in between an insurance office and a nail bar. I had never seen this little shop before so I assumed it must be new. I looked in the window and saw it sold hundreds of different crystals. When I arrived at work I jumped online to have a look at the shop and to my surprise, it turned out it had been there for years. I had to question myself. I'd driven past it hundreds of times and never spotted it. How was that possible?

How had I never noticed it? Why did I suddenly catch sight of it on that particular day, shortly after I had been speaking about crystals? The shop had always been there, or at least as long as I had been driving past it.

The crystal shop is just one example of the many things I drove past every day without even realising they were there. Everything from bike stands, lampposts and the flowers in the window above the shop next door to the droopy curtains in the flat opposite, your unconscious mind is taking in every single bit. Remember, we are processing 11 million bits per second, so if you were to compare that to even the latest smartphone with an impressive memory capacity, taking in the same amount of information as we do, it would be full in no time at all. We manage to go through our entire lives with a constant stream of data to deal with, and so our mind helps us out, to make sure we don't go crazy!

To be able to handle all the external stuff that is consistently inundating our senses, we have a set of internal filters. These filters very kindly help you to literally filter through all of that data and decide what is and what is not on the list!

The List Filter

Many years ago, a friend of mine was getting married, and boy did she have the wedding of the year planned. The more planning she did, the more the wedding seemed to grow. The guest list got bigger each week until the point she wasn't even sure who half the people on it were. It became unmanageable. It was too much for her to take in and so her mind started to filter itself down. She started to forget some of the people she'd invited. When guests had forgotten to specify their meal preference on their RSVPs, she thought they weren't coming to the wedding. With so many different groups of people from different sides of the family and different friend groups, she had merged them all into one another. Her experience of the wedding and the people attending was so different to what was actually happening because of how she had filtered the experience.

Your mind uses its magical mind filters in three different ways to whittle things down. These filters are designed to make your life easy, to take away the gigantic overload of the outside world and make it manageable. They do this through a process of deletion, distortion and generalisation. This is taken from the NLP model of communication, which explains how we filter our reality.

Let's dive into the three different filters and how they each work, so you have a better understanding of the gatekeeper's criteria for what makes it onto the list.

Deletion

Most of the information coming in through your senses is completely deleted out of your awareness, in that you don't even register it. You quite literally don't see things that are right in front of your eyes because your filters have deleted them from your world because they are not important to you in that moment. To make it simple to understand, let me give you an example of deletion in action, a scenario that you've probably experienced in some form or another yourself…

Three people enter the same room for a course on making the perfect pizza dough. After leaving the training room, they are all given a questionnaire to complete. One of the questions within the questionnaire is not about the training content or the course itself, it's about things that were around them in the room.

The question is, how many plants were there in the training room?

Person One answers: *"There were plants? I thought this was about food! I can't say I noticed any. I'm going to have to say none."*

Person Two answers: *"Two or three, I think? Maybe more, I'm not too sure."*

Person Three answers: *"There was a peace lily, a fiddle-leaf fig, two aloe vera plants and a pink orchid."*

All three people were in the same room at the same time, yet they all answered the question very differently. Here is where it gets interesting, because at least one of the plants was directly in their eyeline but their own internal filters will have determined whether or not they were aware of the plants. If plants are important to a person, they will have been brought into their conscious awareness. The RAS will have sent a signal to their brain to say, *"Look over here. There's a plant."* If plants are not important, then they may well have looked directly at the plant and still not consciously registered it. The gatekeeper will have decided this 'plant' isn't on the list and so it's not getting in!

Whilst this is an isolated story that probably has very little impact in the grand scheme of things, think about it in terms of the whole of life. How many opportunities, people and experiences that could help you to create the life you really want are you completely oblivious to because they've been deleted from your experience?

What are you not aware of that, if you were, would be the answer to the question you may not have asked yet?

Distortion

If you've ever been given something that was intended to be a compliment but you took as an insult, then you'll have an idea of how distortion works. When you mistake something for something it is not, your perception of reality has been distorted.

I remember as a child being absolutely certain that every time I heard a floorboard creak, there was a burglar in the house! Whilst this wasn't true, in my reality, in that moment, it was and my body would respond to it. My heart would race. I imagined someone sneaking around the house wearing a balaclava and I felt scared. I was experiencing it as though it was real.

I had taken the sound of the creaky floorboard and distorted it into being something completely different. This doesn't just apply to children with highly active imaginations; it's something that happens to all of us every second of the day. Someone could be genuinely offering you help or guidance but through your filters, you interpret it as them showing off and so you dismiss it. There could be an opportunity staring you in the face that will propel your goals forward and you view it as a scam, looking for the catch – it's too good to be true. Disclaimer here: that doesn't mean there aren't scams out there; it does mean there could be times where what is being offered to you is being met with resistance because of a distorted perception of it.

If you were to look at things through a different lens, what else could they be?

Generalisation

One of the ways that you handle all of the information coming in is to unconsciously categorise it into groups, to make it more manageable. For example, each time you see a moving vehicle, you don't have to think about whether it's a car, motorbike, bus, lorry, etc. You know these are all examples of vehicles and therefore they move and take people from one place to another. If you didn't generalise information, then every time you saw a moving vehicle, you would have to think about what was in front of you. Just imagine, for a moment, if you weren't able to categorise 'cars' as being 'cars', and every time you saw a different make, model, colour, engine size and so on, you had to consciously think about it as being something completely new... there would be little room to do anything else. Thank goodness you are able to generalise information!

Generalisations are also the basis of beliefs. Let me give you an example of this: take a child who passes their spelling test and is then told by their parents and teachers that they are so clever and good at tests. Bravo! That child could take what they have been told and believe it is true, and so a belief has been formed that they are clever and good at tests.

Years later, when they may be taking a whole range of different tests, they apply this belief to everything they do. They generalise the information across many different areas of their life. Whether it's a driving test, a piano exam or something they deem a person needs to be clever for, like learning a new language, they have generalised the belief that they can do anything. Pretty useful!

Of course, like anything, there is a flip side and many people generalise events and create beliefs that aren't empowering too. Another child may fail a test and then apply not being clever enough to everything they do, concluding that they are a failure. Whether good or bad, wanted or unwanted, generalisations are powerful at influencing our perception of reality as we know it.

Time to bring this together and give you an idea of what's going on outside of you versus how you are experiencing it from the inside. Continuing with the theory of NLP, from the 11 million bits of information that your unconscious mind is taking in every second of the day, you filter it down to make it manageable for your conscious mind to process through deleting, distorting and generalising. Now, here's the bit that's worth paying attention to... From those 11 million bits, you whittle it down and are left with a much smaller amount and that smaller amount is the part you are aware of, that information is what your conscious mind notices. Here's the crazy part: from those 11 million bits per second, you are only left with and aware of approximately 126 bits of information every second.

WOAH... How much?

Imagine you're in a stadium with 11 million seats all filled with people. In any second of time, you would only know that 126 of those people sat in seats exist. Your unconscious mind is taking in the other 10,999,874, but the gatekeeper isn't letting them in. Their names aren't on the list and so they are staying outside.

Apply this to your life for a moment and think about how many opportunities are happening right in front of you every second of the day that you aren't aware of. The answers to all of your questions are ready and available for you. All you have to do is change what you let in and what stays out.

Which begs the question, how does your brain decide which 126 bits it will let through the gate?

The 126 bits you are left with, the information you perceive in your world, is filtered through your unconscious mind, where your beliefs, values, personality type, memories, concepts about the world, your attitude and everything that makes up you and your version of reality. This is the reason why your unconscious mind holds so much power – as mentioned in Chapter 3, 95% of what you do happens without you even thinking about it; 95% of the thoughts you have, the things you say to yourself, the behaviours you carry out, the way you feel, all happens on autopilot. When you make changes to the programming that runs the unconscious mind, the filters are adjusted and the things you delete, distort and generalise in your experience will be different. The world outside you is like a projector reflecting back at you the world inside of you. When you change your thinking, you change your focus.

Acclaimed author and screenwriter James Redfield said, "Where attention goes, energy flows." Attention is your focus and it's the very thing that activates your RAS.

Here's an overview of how your focus and attention work in relation to your RAS. There are three different factors that your RAS is activated by and searches for.

1. **The things you deem important. These are influenced by your deepest motivators, preferences and beliefs and are stored in your unconscious mind. They are the programs you are running in your metaphorical submarine.**

2. **Your name. Sounds simple, yet this is why you can be in a crowded room of people and still hear your name mentioned in a conversation that's taking place a few feet away from you.**

3. **Whether or not your partner wants sex. Really? It's true! That piece of information filters its way through all of the other noise, so no matter what else is going on around you, you just know when they are feeling frisky!**

Your RAS is doing you a massive favour. It's lightening the load and doing all the heavy lifting for you. Just think how much energy and mind power it would take if you had to sit with your list and filter through everything. It would be exhausting to the point that you would get nothing else done.

Your job is to use your conscious mind to train your RAS in knowing what weights to lift. You want to direct its focus to spot the very things you are looking for and keep out all the distractions that are in opposition to it. When you master that, the life you desire is reflected back at you in all its glory.

If you don't like what you see, or you want something different, you need to begin changing your attention and focus.

Let's bring back the red car for a moment.

As soon as your attention is aimed towards a particular thing, your RAS is activated whenever that thing is present, hence the reason why when you decide you want a certain car, or anything else for that matter, you see it everywhere. It's not a coincidence; it's the science of your brain!

Follow along with the short exercise below to experience very briefly how the RAS works.

- **Firstly, look around you right now and notice the colour blue. Actively look for it and as you do, notice how much blue you can see.**

- **Now, close your eyes and say to yourself the word 'red' at least 10 times. When you open your eyes, notice how much redder everything looks. Notice how your attention is drawn to everything red that you can find.**

- **The colours in the room were always the same, yet because of your focus, your RAS jumped into action and was activated to look for a particular thing: the colour red.**

The best way to decide what the gatekeeper lets in is to create the list you want. Be the boss of your own RAS.

Time to get focused!

Chapter 5
The Power of Focus

Intention plants the seed for what is to come.

Intention is a powerful thing; it directs your focus and energy. When you set an intention, there is an energetic charge behind it that is more powerful than wishing, hoping or dreaming. It has the potential to move things in the direction you want, activating your RAS to home in on and consciously bring what you are seeking to your awareness.

"Seek and you shall find"
Matthew 7:7

This quote states that if you actively look for something, you will find it.

To give you a little science behind why intention is so powerful, I'm going to give you a very brief overview of quantum physics and how it affects our external world. Bear with me here…

We live in a world of energy, which consists of waves and particles. Waves transport energy from one place to another. They're not localised and they are not something you can point at or hold in your hand. They move and create patterns, much like the wave of ripples that form in water when you throw a stone in. Particles, on the other hand, are solid matter – what we see, hear and experience in our reality. They are localised and so you are able to point at them. They move in a linear way.

Those waves of energy consist of an energetic field of possibility. All and every possibility that could take place exists in a waveform and at any moment in time there are multiple choices, multiple realities, that we have the opportunity to experience.

Everything that could exist, does exist!

The thing that turns those waves of possibility into a particle – in other words, what turns the possibility of something being real into reality itself – is our observation of it. When we observe something, we bring it into our existence.

From all of those waves and all the possibilities they bring, there is the wave that is most likely to materialise. This is known as the wave of probability, the most likely version of reality that you will experience. Listen up because this is where intention comes in.

Your intention directly impacts your focus and it is your focus on a particular thing that takes it from being a wave of possibility and turns it into physical matter, your reality. The observation of the wave turns it into a particle (the physical matter stuff you can touch). The act of consciously observing it makes the wave of potentiality and collapses it into a particle. Observing something or focusing on it actualises it in your world.

If you go looking for something, you will find it.

If this has piqued your interest, I encourage you to do your own research to discover more. There are many experiments that have been carried out over the years including the famous double-slit experiment by Thomas Young in 1802. I recommend popping 'double-slit experiment' in your search engine if you're keen to find out more.

Whatever you decide to do in life, the important thing to know is that your intention will direct your focus, which increases the likelihood of it happening. It takes all of those possible realities and whittles them down to the most probable. The most probable being the one that has the most energy flowing towards it.

Let me give you a really simple example so you can understand intention in this context. Imagine you are on a boat and in that boat, there are 50 cabins. You are informed that 25 of the cabins are run-down with no luxuries, just the basic necessities to accommodate you.

The other 25 cabins are quite the opposite. They have been upgraded to give you an experience fit for royalty.

However, you don't know which cabin is which. Your only job is to choose which cabin door you will go through.

This is where intention becomes really important. There are multiple waves of possibility, or multiple doors you can choose from, and your intention and focus will influence the decision you make when choosing which door to take. Of all of the waves of possibility, all the cabins available, the one that you actually open the door to will be influenced by your intention.

That doesn't mean that having the intention of choosing a cabin of luxury guarantees that you will. It also doesn't mean that it won't, but it does mean that you can intend to have the experience you desire regardless. If you decided that you'll only be happy if you choose a cabin of luxury, then the experience you do have is out of your hands as you're no longer in control of how you feel. The response is dictated by external events.

Think back to the universal Law of Cause and Effect: living a life at the mercy of whatever is thrown your way, placing any responsibility for your life outside of you, which leaves you powerless to do anything about it.

If you intend on having a great time and being the one who is responsible for this, regardless of what cabin you end up in, you will have a very different experience to relying on the cabin to deliver. Your intention will influence the experience you have of whichever cabin you choose.

Setting an intention to have an amazing time will activate your RAS to notice all the amazing possibilities wherever you end up and you will filter your reality accordingly. Your RAS is on high alert to bring to your attention the very things that you have decided are important and you are focused on.

If you intend to have a wonderful time and you happen to open the door to the run-down cabin, your RAS will find all the ways it is wonderful. You may then see the room as a place of solitude, without distraction, or somewhere you can relax and enjoy being away from the busyness of the world.

When you approach life with the intention that your reaction will be dependent on whatever is put in front of you, you may not even end up enjoying or even noticing the luxuries when you do open the door to them.

Always make sure you set your intention in a way that directs your focus towards what you want to create.

Asking Better Questions

A simple way to change the direction of your focus and improve your life is to ask better questions. The questions you ask yourself will activate your RAS to find the answers.

Think of your RAS like your very own internet search engine. The questions you ask are the answers you will find. I spent many years asking myself, why me? Why can't I… make money, find a man who loves me for who I am, make friends, feel happy, find a career I love, get a job… Fill in your own blank! So many things came from a place of lack, scarcity and a belief that nothing would change.

Asking myself those questions provided me with the answers to them. I continually found evidence that supported the reasons why I would never be a success, make money, have a happy relationship, feel as good as other girls. The more evidence I gathered, the more I believed it to be true. My RAS continually brought to my attention everything I was focused on. The problem back then was my intention. Whilst it's not my proudest moment, on some level, I wanted those things to be true. If I could prove to myself and others that I didn't have what it takes, that it wasn't my fault, it was the cards I was dealt and the universe kept showing me that what I was saying was true, then my fate was out of my hands and I didn't have to take responsibility for my life. I was so scared that if I took a leap of faith, I would fail and so I kept myself safe by playing small. If I didn't go for anything, then I couldn't get it wrong.

The problem with this is that it didn't stop me wanting those things. After years of kidding myself and pretending that life was better without the risk of messing up, I had a realisation. I was actually a Jedi Master of creating my reality. I'd become so good at finding the answers to the questions I was asking myself that it was almost scary. I would only have to ask myself, why was I so rubbish at everything I did? Why could I never succeed at anything? What did I have to offer in a relationship? And often that same day the evidence would come flying at me. I would have job applications rejected or my partner would cheat on me and actually tell me the person he cheated with was much prettier, had more money or was better in some kind of way. I looked for the answers and I found them. It dawned on me that if I could do that, then surely I could create the things I actually wanted. I thought that I was rubbish at focusing, when the opposite was actually true. I had just gotten so good at focusing on what I didn't want my life to be.

I'd love to say that having that realisation changed everything overnight but the truth is that, like anything in life, it takes practice. An easy place to start is by changing the questions you ask yourself. Make it your intention to ask better questions and find better answers.

Turn the 'why can't I/haven't I/don't I?' questions into a 'how can I?' question. That question alone will dramatically increase the possibility of a solution coming your way. Asking *why* questions can encourage rationalisations for why you find yourself in a certain position. That's the conscious mind kicking in as a protection mechanism. Asking *how, where, who* and *what* questions will activate your RAS to run those questions through its filters and put your mind on high alert whenever an answer is present. It will look for all the ways *how, where, who* and *what* for you.

How can I... make the money I want, find a good man, start losing weight, set up my own business, travel the world, learn a new hobby?

Where can I find...?

Who can help with...?

What can I do about... *being a unique life coach?*

This can also be used when you notice yourself making statements that are limiting you from achieving what you want.

"I can't do it", *"I'll never have..."*, *"I don't know how to..."*

Instead, turn them into a question of

"How can I do it?"

"How can I have.. a" happy healthy life/work balance?

"How can I learn to... work smarter not harder?

"What do I have?"

One Thought at a Time

When you change your thoughts, you change your life and there are some thoughts that you have probably been thinking for what feels like FOREVER! The thoughts that are deeply embedded and ingrained into your unconscious, the ones that feel like they are stuck for good and no amount of positive thinking will shift.

Well, if you were hoping to be excused at this point, to see yourself as the exception, then I'm sorry to be the one to disappoint you. Those deeply embedded thoughts hold no more power than new thoughts and beliefs you created a week ago. The only difference is that you have been thinking them for much longer and so the connections in your mind are well rehearsed.

Because of this, when a new thought comes along that contradicts it, the old way of thinking has the advantage of power in its corner. Labelling these long-term thoughts and beliefs as being more significant reinforces them and gives them power. There will be thoughts that have a much bigger impact on your life than others, but either way they are just thoughts, and thoughts can be changed.

It's the world of paradox – a thought is nothing more than a thought; it's not real, and yet thinking something makes it real, so therefore it is the most powerful thing.

Think of your thoughts like footprints in the snow. The ones you have been thinking for some time have created a pathway that you walk along often and so the ground is well trodden. This is the same in your mind. When you keep thinking thoughts, the connections in your brain keep firing over and over again, which makes it easier for them to do it each time. Your unconscious mind's primary role is to keep you safe and so it likes the familiar and it always looks for the easiest route for you to get where you are going to. Even though the thoughts you keep thinking may not be serving you, they are known, so they feel comfortable. They also take very little effort, because you have thought them so many times before and so your mind will go to those thoughts first as they are the path of least resistance, the easy route.

The first time you think a new thought, it's like creating a new pathway in the snow. There is no obvious route; the steps will usually feel a little harder to begin with and there may be more effort required as you haven't walked that way before. Walking in thick untrodden snow can be hard work. The easier option is the one where you keep walking on the path that is worn in; but, if that way of thinking isn't getting you what you want in life, then is it really the easiest option or does it actually make life harder?

A life of regret is hard; a life of feeling unfulfilled is hard; a life you don't enjoy waking up to is hard. When you look at it like that, thinking new thoughts is absolutely the better option and something you can do.

When you keep walking the new path consistently and focusing on thinking new thoughts, eventually that becomes the path most trodden and the old path, the old way of thinking, is filled with snow and it's no longer the easiest route to walk; those old thoughts are no longer the easiest to think. The new embedded thoughts become your new default and so you start thinking them automatically.

Doing this process consciously will take a little time and practice, but one thing that's for sure is the time will pass anyway. You're always going to have thoughts, so you might as well start changing those unwanted ones. Whilst the concept of creating your reality is often focused on the physical manifestations, the real reason to do any of this stuff, any self-improvement, is because it feels good! Thinking negative thoughts feels rubbish, so it makes complete sense to begin to change them. If you're reading this book, the chances are you have a desire to make changes and probably live a more enhanced life than the one you're currently living. My guess is that the reason you want to change it is because of the way you think you will feel when it arrives. Waiting for something outside of you to change how you feel inside is being at the effect of it. It's using the reasoning that the stuff will cause me to feel good, which puts responsibility for your feelings outside of you. If, instead, you set an intention for what you want and then concentrate on feeling good regardless of the stuff, your focus is on the receiving of it, and the wave of potential is more likely to turn into the wave of probability through your observation of it.

Easy to say, right? But where do you begin when the thoughts you currently have are miles apart from the thoughts you want to have? The easiest way to begin changing them so you start to feel good right now is by taking it one thought at a time!

Without the small things, the big things would not exist; never underestimate their importance and power.

Jumping from a negative, ingrained thought to a new, positive one that is so far removed and feels completely out of reach tends not to work so well. The gap is too big and the current thought fights to stay put, reaffirming its truth.

If you've spent years, maybe a whole lifetime, telling yourself you're not worthy or you'll never be rich, then thinking *I am worthy, I am rich* is just too much of a leap. Even if it isn't serving you, your mind wants to protect you, and that thought or belief is what it knows and so it feels safe.

We all have to start from wherever we are right now, so rather than beating yourself up for not being where you think you should be, fighting the thought or pushing against it, instead accept that it's just where you are, not where you're going, and be kind to yourself.

Then, take one step at a time!

To begin changing an unwanted, negative thought that is far from your new desired, positive thought, you need to bridge the gap. You do this by creating stepping-stones to the new way of thinking by reaching for something that is slightly more towards the thought you want and something you can believe, taking you in the direction of the new thought a little bit at a time.

Changing a thought, even just a little, has a compound effect on everything you do and it's something that anyone can do immediately. The key then is consistency!

ACTIVATION POINT – Bridging the Gap

In the previous activation point, Becoming Aware, you made a note of the thoughts that aren't serving you and what you want instead.

Using the list you created, identify which ones seem far out of reach and carry out the following steps.

- **Create four columns as below:**

Current Thought	Step One	Step Two	Desired Thought

- **Fill in the unwanted current thought and the desired thought column using your list.**

    Here are some examples:

Current Thought	Step One	Step Two	Desired Thought
I always say the wrong thing.			I always know what to do and say.
I'll never be successful.			I am successful.
All the good men are taken.			There are many great men available who are perfect for me

- **Bridge the gap.**

  Create at least two or even three thoughts that take you from the current to the desired thought. Each stepping-stone should be a step rather than a jump towards the new thought and this may be just a slight improvement.

  Each step must be one that you can get on board with. It may not be something you are thinking yet, but it must be a thought that you think is believable. If the step is slightly smaller than you would like to begin with, that's okay — it's still a step in the right direction.

  Here are some examples:

Current Thought	Step One	Step Two	Desired Thought
I always say the wrong thing.	There are occasions where I say the right thing. OR I sometimes say the wrong thing but not always.	There are many times when I've known the right thing to say. OR I trust myself to say the right thing most of the time.	I always know what to do and say.

I'll never be successful.	Everyone starts somewhere. I'm beginning to head in the right direction. OR Maybe I could be successful.	I'm becoming more successful every day. OR Success is a journey, one that I am on.	I am successful.
All the good men are taken.	A lot of the good men are taken but not all of them. OR I only want one man and I'm sure there is at least one good one that's still available.	There are a number of good men out there for me. OR I am enjoying getting to know men and finding there are a number of good ones.	There are many great men available who are perfect for me.

- **Practise the new thought.**

  Once you have your list of stepping-stones, it's time to put them into practice, starting with the first new thought.

Catching yourself in the moment may sound easier than it is because most of what we do is unconscious; we're not even aware of some of our thoughts.

Really begin to pay attention to your thoughts and how you are feeling. If you're feeling rubbish, then I can guarantee you're thinking a negative thought.

Every time you notice that you are thinking an unwanted thought, in that very moment, start by saying to yourself, either in your head or out loud if possible,

"That's okay."

You are interrupting the thought, letting your unconscious mind know that it's safe and giving yourself a break all in one go. Then, take a deep breath and say to yourself,

"I've got this and I know [insert the new thought]."

You're reassuring yourself. And the truth is, you have got this. I believe in you!

If that thought feels too far out of reach, again, it's okay. It's all feedback and you can just create a stepping-stone before that one that is slightly less of a jump.

Remember, the important part is that it's something you can get on board with.

- **Affirm the new thought.**

  Time to take the new thought to the next level!

Set an alarm or a reminder on your phone every hour, two hours, three hours… as often as you can (but no longer than four).

When the alarm goes off, check in with how you are feeling and take a moment to honour that feeling. Congratulate yourself for taking the time to acknowledge and become conscious of your thoughts.

Take a second to remind yourself of the new thought, the next stepping-stone. Think about that thought and imagine how life is when that new thought is true. Notice what you see, hear, feel and know.

Once you have that feeling, turn up the dial, increase the better-feeling thought to twice the intensity, then three times the intensity. Focus on it and really indulge in that feeling.

- **Set your intention**

  Now, set an intention for the hours between now and your next alarm.

  Set the intention to continue to focus your thoughts on the stepping-stone and in the direction of your desired thought.

- **Repeat**

  When the next alarm goes off, take a minute to notice how different you felt over the previous hours. Be aware of the things that you have perceived in a new light and how your thinking is beginning to change, even if only for a minute here or there… It's still progress!

It will take repetition to create those new thought connections in your mind. Each time you think the new thought, you are walking in those new footprints in the snow so it may take some work and practice to remind yourself to do it.

Give yourself a pat on the back for taking the time to do this exercise. This is the work of changing your reality from the inside out. Imagine how differently you will feel a year from now when you do this every day!

Remember to always ask yourself *how* you can instead of *why* you can't!

Chapter 6
Physical Manifestation

*"The day you plant the seed is not
the day you eat the fruit."*
Fabienne Fredrickson

You've set your intention; you know what you want; you've thought about it, imagined it happening, maybe taken some action towards it, so where the hell is it?

After months and months of spending time every day picturing my new red car sitting on my driveway, seeing my hands on the steering wheel, imagining all the trips I would take in it and feeling how good it was to own it, I really felt as though the car should have been mine already. When you ask, it is given, right? And I had certainly asked, more than once!

That being said, if I'm honest there was a little something about the whole 'ask and it is given' concept that bothered me. I couldn't quite comprehend how when you ask for something, it is done and the universe creates it in an instant. The theory didn't make any sense to me in the real physical day-to-day life. Rationally, I knew that I couldn't just ask for a car, open my eyes and it would appear on the drive with the keys pushed through the letterbox. I accepted on some level that all of the things I wanted were out there somewhere ready for me to attract, but if it was already done, I struggled to understand where it was and why I hadn't received it the moment I asked for it. I spent my days wondering where my car was, guessing how it would arrive and how long it would take. I tried thinking of all the ways it could come to me, from winning a competition, inheriting it from some long-lost relative I knew nothing of, a family member winning some money and buying me one. I was limited by the options that I thought were a possibility, albeit a very slight one. This left me feeling confused and discouraged.

What I came to learn in later years gave me the answers I had been looking for, explaining why the car hadn't fallen from the sky and onto my driveway. The part of the equation, which isn't much of a surprise but I didn't know back then, is that there is a time delay involved in the creation process of turning thoughts into physical stuff, a process that we are all participants in. When I heard this I was pleased to discover I wasn't going mad! It gave me a massive sense of relief. I was finally able to give myself a break when material goods didn't land on my door an hour after deciding I wanted them.

The delay in receiving the physical things you have asked for can easily be one of the most frustrating parts of creating your reality if you let it be, or it can also be the most exciting part.

My experience back then was one of frustration and annoyance which, in hindsight, explains why I was not getting anywhere fast in bringing the things I desired to me. I wasn't looking forward to them. I was angry they weren't there and I felt the lack of them. Had I appreciated that there can be a time lag between thinking and creation, I may have had fewer questions and enjoyed the process more. It really is something to get excited about, especially once you accept that the length of time it takes really is down to you. You are the one responsible for, and therefore in control of, how quickly your life changes.

The timescales involved in physical manifestation vary from person to person based on their starting point, their reality as they currently experience it and their ability to see past it. However, I'm going to share with you some guidelines and the factors that speed up or slow down the lag between asking and receiving. To explain the manifestation journey, the timescales to physical fruition and how to get there, we're going to continue a little more into the world of the quantum field. Hold on tight!

Energy of Creation

Earlier on, we touched on how the world we live in is made up of waves and particles. We essentially live in two different worlds that are linked and interact with each other: the quantum and the physical.

The quantum world is the energetic world of waves, which includes every thought and feeling that we have. On the other hand, the physical world is made up of particles, the stuff that we know about and interact with through our senses: what we see, hear, touch, smell and taste.

Everything that exists in the physical world was first created energetically in the quantum realm. Nothing in our physical world would exist without the thought that preceded it.

This is easy to understand when it comes to the creation of some things, for example, a car. If there wasn't a thought about the car, followed by the design of it and the steps that follow, then there would be no car. This is a physical creation that can easily be reverse engineered, but creation is not limited to the cars that exist; the principle is true for all manifestation.

Every creation happens energetically before it happens physically – every relationship, all the money, the opportunities, the connections, the cars and everything else that you experience in this multi-dimensional reality called life.

What many people don't realise, or even forget, is that we are always creating our reality, every second of every day. It's just that most people do it by accident rather than design. I certainly used to hold the mindset that I created some things in my life but not others and I'm sure you can guess which kind of experiences I preferred to not take responsibility for. I thought manifestation was only about what we quite literally asked for, preferably out loud or by writing it on paper. The truth is that everything, and I mean everything, we have experienced in our lives was and always will be created by us. Going back to the universal Law of Cause and Effect again: for every effect, every manifestation, there will have been something that caused it. When we accept this, we take responsibility for everything in our life – the good and the not-so-good. Whilst it may not be a popular way of thinking, it's the only way that we are able to do something to change it. The journey of creating your reality is about learning how to do it on purpose rather than life happening by default whilst you're busy doing other things and running on autopilot.

Let's go a little deeper into both the energetic and the physical worlds to give you a better understanding of the access you have to them, the relationship between the two and how that impacts on the things you manifest.

Two Worlds

The quantum world is the energetic world where things happen straightaway. There is no time involved. This is the world where 'ask and it is given' applies. Once a thought has been put out into the energy field, it exists as a wave of possibility, meaning there is a possibility that it will manifest. The process that turns the thought wave into physical matter is the observation of, or focusing on, it.

You have probably heard the question of whether or not a tree that falls in the woods makes a sound when no one is around. In quantum physics the answer would be no, because unless someone observes it happening, it doesn't exist in their reality. Sounds are an interpretation of vibration and to interpret something, it has to come through at least one of our five senses. The very act of observing and measuring something is what turns a wave of potential into a particle.

Absolutely everything in the entire universe starts out as a wave and that wave is measured in cycles. Each cycle consists of an up and down where the wave reaches its peak (the highest point) and trough (the lowest point). The wavelength is measured by the completion of a cycle, which is the distance between the peak of one wave to the peak of the next and the distance between the trough of one wave to the trough of the next.

Think of it like a wave in the ocean hitting its crest before it comes back down again, falling below the surface of the ocean where it hits the lowest point, before working its way back up again (see Image 1).

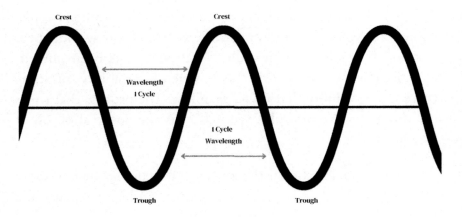

Image 1

Your thoughts and feelings emit a wave and each wave vibrates at a certain frequency. Frequency quite simply refers to how often something happens or, in this case, how frequently the wave completes a full cycle.

To recap from the universal Law of Vibration, higher-frequency waves have more cycles per second; lower-frequency waves have fewer cycles per second. The lower the frequency, the more dense and solid things appear. Particles are very low-frequency waves vibrating at such a slow rate that they appear to be solid matter.

Everything is energy; everything vibrates! It's the Law of Vibration.

Everything includes you; it includes all of us. For every thought we think and the way we feel about those thoughts, we are emitting a wave that has its own frequency. High-frequency feelings are those such as peace, joy and love, and they feel light in their energy; the frequency or the rate at which they vibrate is faster. They have a high number of wave cycles per second, so each wave cycle follows the next very closely.

Low-frequency feelings such as grief, guilt, sadness and despair all feel heavy in their energy; the frequency at which they vibrate is much slower. They have a lower number of wave cycles per second; the waves are longer – they have a bigger gap between each of them; they don't follow as closely together. They feel denser; there is a gravitation pull and so the weight of them can be felt.

You can feel this energy when you meet people who you may term as 'high vibe'. The energy they emit feels different because it is quite literally lifted in comparison to lower vibrational energy.

Good-feeling high-frequency waves vibrate at a faster rate than bad-feeling low-frequency waves. There is more energy and momentum behind them and so things happen more quickly, which brings us to how this relates to the time it takes to create physical manifestations!

This model is based on many studies I have come across, including the work of Joe Dispenza, Gregg Braden and Peter Sage who are true experts in their field. I've modelled the graph below on Peter Sage's talk 'The Art of Living in Through Me'. It shows a visual representation of waves and the frequency at which they vibrate, demonstrating the link between the frequency in relation to the timescales involved between thoughts and things.

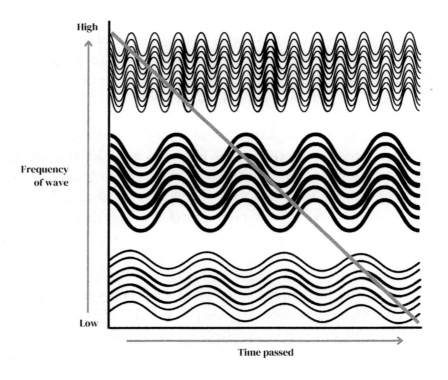

Image 2

On the vertical axis, you'll see the frequency rate of the wave, starting with a low frequency at the bottom of the axis to a high frequency at the top.

The higher the frequency, the more frequently a full wave cycle is completed. This results in there being more wave cycles per second. The lower the frequency, the less frequently a full wave cycle is completed and so there are fewer wave cycles per second. The higher frequencies have a smaller gap between wave cycles than the lower frequencies.

On the horizontal axis, there is a representation of the time it takes for a wave to transform into a particle, or a thought to turn into a thing.

When a person is vibrating at a low frequency, when they feel those low vibrational emotions, there are fewer wave cycles per second and therefore a bigger gap between each wave. The fewer the number of cycles per second, the longer it takes to create physical results. When a person is vibrating at a higher frequency, when they feel those high-vibration emotions, there are more wave cycles per second and so there is less of a gap between each wave, and so the time to physical creation is less.

There is a tipping point in time whereby energy turns into matter, a point at which the quantum world meets the physical world and those thoughts become things. This is known as the Quantum to Newtonian transition point. The timescales of that tipping point, of taking something from the energetic quantum world in the physical world of matter, has been found to be very similar to the timescales we experience in the physical world. The transition from wave into particle takes place after around four to eight weeks of sustained energy flowing in a single direction. That means that after four to eight weeks of focused energy, there will be evidence of energy turning into physical matter.

Now, anyone who has attempted to create or manifest something in their life that hasn't yet happened may well tell you they have been focused on it for a lot longer than four to eight weeks. I spent years asking for the same things over and over again and they still didn't appear. The key to all of this, and the part I was missing when it came to creation, is the word sustained.

When I used to think about what I wanted, I'd be specific about it. I'd ask for it; I'd write it down – all the things I had read I needed to do. Every day I would sit for between 10 and 30 minutes either meditating or visualising and getting myself into a feeling of already having the things I wanted, and it felt great. My mind would wander at times but I enjoyed my moments picturing the car, the relationship, the money, the friends, the holidays, the life that I wanted. When I'd finished my time of focus, I'd carry on with life and I did feel more positive for having done it. During those 10–30 minutes, I altered the rate of frequency at which my thoughts and feelings vibrated, and in those moments I was speeding up the manifestation process. The number of cycles per second that I was emitting energetically was high. If I'd continued to emit that rate of frequency consistently, if I'd sustained it for a period of six to eight weeks, the physical manifestation of my thoughts and feelings would have become evident.

Looking back now, I realise that I didn't continue to focus on and direct my energy towards all the things I wanted to create when the mundane of the day kicked in. After leaving my meditation chair and resuming normal life, I'd revert back to my default feeling, which was pretty low. I felt the lack of the things I desired. It would only take an argument with my then partner, an unexpected bill coming through the door, my car breaking down or even just getting stuck in traffic and I would fall back into feeling low again, sometimes even lower than before because I had dared to imagine what could be, a feeling so far removed from my then reality. These were things that happened daily rather than once in a while, so it was a regular occurrence. In those moments, my focus was on all the things I didn't have that I wanted. Instead of feeling good, I would find myself thinking that when I have (X), the car, the money... then I'll feel (Y), happy, calm, confident, etc.

I'm going to give myself a break here and if any of this relates, I invite you to do the same because I was doing the best I could at that time, as we all are. Knowing what I know now, I would've done things differently but without those experiences, I wouldn't know what I do today. I also know that in a few years' time, I'll probably look back at the things I'm doing now and wonder, *What was I thinking?* In fact, I plan on that being the case because that is the beauty of growth and hindsight. If you find yourself wishing you'd done things differently in the past and being unkind to yourself for the choices you made, see it as the blessing it truly is. You have learnt from the past, and the future will be better because of it.

During that period, there were times when I'd pull myself up on my negative thinking and make an effort to consciously think more positively, but the problem was that the minute I wasn't consciously holding myself accountable and paying attention to my thoughts, my unconscious thought patterns and emotions kicked in and I was back to my usual default level of feeling. When I stopped trying to row the boat in a different direction, pushing hard on the oars, the submarine carried out the automatic way of thinking, feeling and behaving, and so I reverted back to my default ways of doing things. The day-to-day frequency I felt back then was pretty low most of the time with only the occasional high. I wasn't particularly aware of how bad it felt because I didn't have a lot of experience to compare it to. Life just seemed hard, like a slog, and it had become normal. Getting through the week was the name of the game!

To relate my own personal experience back to energy and manifestation, the frequency I sustained for the majority of the time was a low frequency. Those higher-frequency moments were few and far between in comparison, which is a really important part of the puzzle.

Think of it this way. If someone spends 10, 20, 30 or even 60 minutes a day focusing on the life they want to create and they then spend the other 23 hours of the day thinking about and focusing on the opposite of that, the energy is tipped in favour of and directed towards the unwanted. The word 'sustained' is massively important because it's sustained energy that creates results, and 23 hours a day is pretty sustained. This is also true of spending a week totally focused on what is wanted and then turning the focus to wondering where the physical evidence is. The energy hasn't been sustained for a long enough period and the switch in focus slows down or pauses any momentum that was in play.

Now, this doesn't mean you have to spend 24 hours a day completely and utterly focused at all times on exactly what you want, although if you do that, then you are demonstrating intentional leadership of your life and kudos to you!

Whilst 24 hours of all your attention and focus in one direction is not realistic because we're people living a physical experience, things happen and our focus turns to the unwanted and we feel rubbish, you can absolutely change your internal filters so the majority of the time you see the world through the lens you desire. For everything we desire, its opposite must exist – the other end of the scale. These instances of distraction from what we want are of benefit because they give us contrast and clarity. The key is to take the feedback and switch your focus. The more you practise this, the quicker you will become at it.

If you're still on a journey of learning and growth, which I believe we all are, and you were to spend just 51% of your time focusing your energy on the things you want to create and the other 49% focused on lack, then the scales would tip. They would have to. Spending 51% of your day feeling good and placing your attention on the abundance of what you already have and the joy of knowing what is coming would be a massive shift for most people. It's easier than it first sounds because around six to nine hours each day will actually be spent sleeping, so you only have to focus on feeling good for about nine hours a day. Let me rephrase that: you have the privilege of and can enjoy spending at least nine hours focusing on feeling great just because you can.

Energy is power that can be transformed from one form to another, from waves into particles. In the context of creating your reality, energy is all about your feelings and the power and force behind them. The more intense and good feeling the emotion is, the more energy is present. This is something we have all experienced at some point in our lives. You can set an alarm to wake you up at 3am to catch a flight for your holiday and bounce right out of the bed. When that same alarm goes off at 6am to go to a job that you hate, suddenly that energy has disappeared; it's curled up in a ball under the quilt. In both scenarios, you're waking up, yet the energy behind it is different and the reason it's different is because one feels great and the other maybe not so much.

Focused energy is placing your attention on the feelings that you believe the physical manifestation will give you – being able to generate the energy in advance of creating and receiving what you want, which is really the reason for wanting it in the first place. Feeling good shouldn't be something that feels like a chore and if it does, then maybe the ways you've chosen have been driven by escaping your current reality rather than discovering what feels good for the sheer hell of it!

I mentioned that the timescales can vary and as a guideline, the time it takes to transform something from the quantum energetic world into the physical world are pretty similar to transformations in many physical walks of life. Entrepreneur and human behaviour expert Peter Sage, explains this beautifully; he says that in the metaphysical (or quantum world), we don't have the same reference point that we do in the physical world. Can you imagine going to the gym, having a really great workout and then wondering if, after all that effort, your body will respond? Even though your muscles haven't popped into place straightaway, you wouldn't question if the workout will have any effect; yet so many question whether the creation process works after asking for what they want, because things haven't shown up instantly.

It's accepted in the physical world that our results correspond with our input. In other words, the effects in our life are a consequence of the thoughts and actions that preceded them – the Law of Cause and Effect. If that person who is going to the gym, consistently trained four times a week for four to eight weeks, then the evidence would be visible. The results would vary depending on what that person did during the hours when they were not at the gym, and it's the same in the quantum world. Like a muscle growing, just because the things we are working towards aren't visible immediately, it doesn't mean they aren't transitioning into physical form. When you're changing your body, the things you do outside of the gym matter as much as what you do in the gym. The food you eat, rest, hydration, supplements; these all contribute towards the speed of your results. This translates to all types of manifestation. The things that happen outside of writing the goal – meditating, visualising, etc. – are all factors in the creation process. Everything from where you focus your attention, how you feel, your environment, your behaviour, the action you take. You become what you do consistently.

After four to eight weeks of sustained focus, there will be a shift in the physical world. Those energetic waves will transform into a particle that is evident to you through your senses. The more sustained focus you have, the more energy builds and grows and the quicker the creation happens.

Think of how you spend your time focusing like watering a plant. If you have two plants, one that is the wanted plant and one is the unwanted plant, which plant grows? The answer is the one that you feed. If you continue to feed the unwanted plant, then it will stay strong. If, instead, you focus on feeding the wanted plant, that will be the one that gets stronger and because your energy is focused on feeding the wanted plant, the unwanted will be starved in the process. Over time, the unwanted plant will shrink, making it even harder to focus on.

Choose the plant you feed wisely!

Of course, like anything in life, it takes practice. No matter where you are in your journey, you will find yourself going backwards and forwards with your focus. It's called being human. The more you practise, the easier it gets and your baseline default frequency raises and you become more attuned to the higher good-feeling vibrations. Those feelings then become the very thing you want to experience more of, regardless of the manifestation.

One of the common hold-ups that people have in this process is wanting instant results, which is understandable. If you're anything like me, when you know what you want, you want it yesterday. A great way to overcome this is to find ways to enjoy the journey and celebrate it along the way, just like you would do in life. It's a bit of a cliché but it's true.

Let's relate this to going on holiday. The journey begins by deciding you want to go away. This is followed by looking at destinations, hotels, the activities you will do whilst there, the food, the culture and anything that may be on your list of important criteria. Whilst you're doing this, you're not actually on your holiday but you have started the journey to get there and it's usually an enjoyable one. Once you've decided exactly where you're going, there is potentially some shopping to do – new beachwear, sandals and sun cream to buy. You're still not on your holiday but it's definitely fun. Then comes the packing…

There may be parts that are less enjoyable than others! I know people who relish this task and, like any steps to creation, there will be things you have to do that you savour less than others. A great question to ask yourself when those tasks arrive is, how can I make this fun? Put your favourite music on, dance around whilst you do it, turn it into a party... whatever works. Enjoy the journey. Then, there's going to the airport if you're flying abroad, the duty-free shopping, the flight itself or the car or boat journey. All of these things have to happen before you arrive at your destination and whether you choose to make the most of and find pleasure in them is up to you.

Now, most people probably enjoy much of the holiday process, so here's another example. When someone begins exercising to improve their physical appearance and health and they have a goal in mind, it is possible to also enjoy the progress they make along the way to getting there. If the aim was to lose two stone, this isn't going happen overnight but they will lose more and more weight each week if they are consistent before reaching the two-stone mark and there will be evidence along the way that they are focused in the right direction. No one would expect a two-stone weight loss instantly and it would be very concerning if that ever happened. If, due to some bizarre freak of nature, it did, the reality is that they wouldn't be ready for it; they wouldn't be prepared. They wouldn't have any clothes that fit them for starters; no one around them would recognise them; they wouldn't recognise themselves or know how their new body worked and responded to the things they are used to doing. Their new eating habits and exercise routine wouldn't have been formed to support their new body, and this principle is true of all creation.

Whilst it's easy to think that we want the things we don't have right now, if they were actually given to us straightaway, we wouldn't be equipped to handle them. Even with the holiday, if you were transported to the destination right this second, I would guess there are a number of things that have to happen for you to be ready for it, from shopping, packing, arranging a dog sitter, booking the time off work so you have a job to go back to, maybe you plan on having a bikini wax before you go. There might be things you need to do, things you need to change or consequences in achieving the goal that you haven't considered, both internal and external. If you were ready for them right now, then you would have them. It's about becoming the person you need to be to have the life you want and noticing the changes happening along the way, so when you arrive, it's who you are.

Become the person you need to be to have the life you want!

Your focused energy in a single direction activates your RAS. Your RAS then searches for the things that are a match and activates whenever there is evidence that supports your achievement of it or a way to make it happen. The more you feel it, the more you reveal it, the more you notice and focus on it, the more highly attuned your RAS is. It then becomes a self-fulfilling loop of creation. If it matches your focus, your RAS will let it in; if it doesn't, you won't see it.

You are reprogramming your unconscious mind, the submarine. Your conscious mind, the rowing boat, where you sit day to day, will undoubtedly drift from time to time, focused in one moment and not the next. You may find that the waves push you backwards and forwards but if you continue rowing in the direction of what you want, one day you may notice some land off in the distance, a sign you're heading in the right direction.

The next day you might find something floating on the water next to you – a small box and inside it's filled with valuable items. Those items may come in the form of a person, a job, money, an opportunity, something that is taking you even closer to what you want, evidence you're on track. Celebrate those moments, feel how great they feel and use them to focus even more on your desired outcomes. The fun really is in the journey of becoming the person you want to be.

When you ask, it is already done in the quantum world. The physical world just needs a little time to catch up. The more time you spend in a higher, good-feeling frequency, the quicker the results are each time. Matter is dense energy that appears solid but it is still energy vibrating at a very slow speed and it takes time and sustained focus to turn a wave into a particle. However, that time can be as little as four to eight weeks!

The wave doesn't follow the particle; it's the other way around. In other words, it's not about changing the physical world so you feel good; you feel good and the physical world changes. It's the universal law of correspondence: as within, so without.

The most important part to all of this is the feeling of it. If you spend five hours a day picturing your dreams coming true but you're not really feeling it, the energy and frequency of your thoughts will be reflective of that and so will the results you get. Our thoughts, feelings and how we show up in the world are all linked, so when one changes, the others change too. If your thoughts are truly directed towards a positive outcome, then you will feel good; the body responds to the mind and vice versa. Thinking about the thing you want but imaging yourself without it, or thinking about why you don't have it, isn't focusing on what you want; it's focusing on the lack of it, which is different and emits a different energy.

The waves of energy that transform into particles are always there and always happening. The rate at which the wave turns into matter is determined by how good you feel and how much of your time is spent focused on what you want.

Think about it... you have the potential to see massive, concrete, tangible results in your life within four to eight weeks, if not sooner. If you've already been feeling predominantly great, with little resistance to the things you desire, those timescales can be dramatically reduced. That is something to feel good about!

ACTIVATION POINT – *Getting Prepared*

Uncovering any potential unconscious blockages is fundamental to allow in and receive the very things you desire. Sometimes, there can be unconscious blocks that we are consciously aware of but we pretend they are not there. Pretending something doesn't exist won't change it.

Hold in mind something you want to achieve and answer the questions below. Be totally honest with yourself.

- **What would happen if I achieved it?**
- **What would the positive consequences be?**

- **What would the negative consequences be?**
- **Who do I need to become to allow those things?**
- **What changes do I have to make to become the person I need to be?**

If you identify anything that could prevent you from achieving what you want, ask yourself how you would deal with that situation if it happened. When you know that you are able to deal with it, your unconscious mind will know that it's safe to allow it into your experience.

For example, when I first started running online courses, I really wanted to fill them straightaway. When it didn't happen, I was puzzled. I asked myself those very questions and uncovered that I was unconsciously stopping it from happening because, even though I wanted it, I didn't really have the capacity to handle it. There wasn't the time to fulfil everything that goes with someone new signing up and the other huge tasks already on the agenda at that time. I knew that delivering a great quality service wouldn't have been possible with the resources available and so I blocked it from happening.

Spotting this allowed me to take steps to build systems that eased the workload and then feel totally congruent and aligned with achieving the goal. The next online course filled up very quickly.

Tipping the scales

Ok, so now you've done some deeper work, it's time to have some fun because fun is a good-feeling place to be. Taking yourself and any situation too seriously in and of itself can lower the frequency of it. Being serious turns what could be a light and free feeling into something heavy. Whilst working towards the things you want, also create time every single day to do something that feels good, maybe something you can incorporate into your goals. Put it in your diary!

I've listed some suggestions below and feel free to add in your own:

- **Meditate**
- **Take a hot bubble bath**
- **Walk in nature – connect with how great it feels to be outdoors**
- **Have a massage or facial**
- **Dance to your favourite song**
- **Have your own pamper session**
- **Put your music on loud and sing at the top of your voice**
- **Make a list of all the positive things you have in your life right now no matter how simple they may seem (I bet there are more than you realise)**
- **Spend time with friends who make you belly laugh (if you don't have those friends yet, make it your mission to find them and get excited about meeting them)**

- **Read a good book**
- **Watch your favourite comedy show**

There are so many ways to feel great right now.

Whilst you are on your way to creating what you want, you can certainly enjoy the ride. Feeling miserable doesn't feel good and it slows down the process. Make it your mission to learn how to feel great and practise every day.

Chapter 7
Magical Motivation

*The reason to succeed must be bigger
than the reason to not.*

Motivation, or lack of it, is one of the biggest reasons people give up, often just when things are starting to get good. You work hard, doing all the things you think you should be doing; your foot is on the accelerator and then, for some unknown reason, you begin to put the brakes on or maybe even hit reverse, undoing all of your good work. So, it's back to square one, leaving you feeling like a failure.

I've been there many times and it can feel as though you are driving yourself crazy!

I spent so many years wondering why this was. Why did I destroy all the effort I had put in? What caused me to sabotage my own results? Why was I so motivated when starting out but when I got closer to what I wanted, the motivation wore off? It made no sense, yet it kept happening. I kept doing it.

It didn't matter if it was to do with work, career, money, relationships or my health, the pattern of destruction seemed to be consistent throughout various areas of my life. I would begin to make headway with friendships and then retreat. I would make a payment on my credit card and then spend twice as much. I'd eat healthily and look after myself all week and then go out of my way to consume as much junk food as I possibly could in the space of one sitting. It was exhausting and I wasn't getting anywhere fast!

The day I discovered what was going on and why this was happening I could've cried with relief. First of all, I realised that I wasn't actually going mad and I finally understood one of the patterns of behaviour that I had been running. The thing with patterns of behaviour is that we tend to take them with us wherever we go. What we do in one area of life, we do in all areas of life. The self-destruct button wasn't confined to a single problem; it spanned across many. Self-sabotage was probably the only thing that was consistent about my inconsistent motivation!

At first glance, recognising that this pattern of hitting self-destruct ran across various parts of my life may have seemed negative, because I was sabotaging my own results in so many different ways. There were different people, different scenarios, different outcomes, yet the theme of self-sabotage was consistent throughout, but simply reframing what it meant changed my whole perception. If there was a pattern, a theme, running in so many parts of my life that were producing the very results I didn't want, if I changed that pattern in one area, surely it would translate in a positive way to the other areas too. This took it from being ALL of these problems that felt overwhelming to think about, down to working on the pattern itself by applying it to just one area, the one causing the most problems and knowing that will positively influence everything else in my life. That was something I could get on board with!

Before getting stuck into the detail of which area of your life would have the most impact on all other areas if you changed it, let me go through the process of motivation, where it comes from and why it doesn't last.

First things first, it's important to understand that motivation is not a magical skill that some have and some don't. There isn't a pill you can take that gives you motivation either. I remember watching people who had what I wanted and wishing I could have their motivation to go and get it. I thought it was something they were born with; they just happened to be part of a lucky group of people who were born into a club that I didn't make it into, and that was the excuse I told myself for many years. The problem, aside from reinforcing the belief that I didn't have what it takes to be successful, was that nothing changed. I was totally on the effect side of life, blaming my genetics for where I'd ended up and I can promise you that digging the hole of reasons why it wouldn't work for me only made it a bigger hole to get out of.

The good news is that motivation isn't something you are either born with or without; it's something we all have. It's just not necessarily driven by the things we like or would like to achieve.

Let's start with looking at where our motivation actually comes from. This is based on the work of the late Dr Tad James, the creator of Time Line Therapy®, and Dr Adriana James, both Master Trainers and experts in the field of NLP hypnotherapy and coaching. Now, believe it or not, the things that motivate us as adults have usually been decided before we reach the tender age of around 10 years old, if not sooner. Back when we were young, we were a little unconscious mind absorbing the world around us, with no conscious mind critically looking at the information we were taking in. The rational logical filter we have as adults hadn't developed up to that period and so we just accepted what we were told to be true and important.

Our well-intended parents, teachers, friends, grandparents, siblings, culture, even fictional TV or book characters, all influenced our views of the world, even without words.

Behaviour speaks volumes!

The way a person behaves is a direct reflection of what is important to them. The things that are important to us are our values – the true motivators for everything we do as people.

The thing with values is that they aren't simply those things we aspire to have. If only it was that straightforward…

"I want to be successful and make money, therefore I am naturally driven to do the things that will help me achieve those things."

If values worked in that way, then we would all achieve everything we ever wanted. Wanting something to be important, to be motivated by that very thing, doesn't make it so. Our values are not something we consciously decide.

Our values reside in our unconscious mind, the submarine!

The way to spot someone's true unconscious values is by how they spend their time. Our values are quite literally the things we value, and so we put them first.

If someone says exercise is important, yet they never make the time to do any, you can assume it's probably not a value of theirs, even if they want it to be. If it was truly something they value highly, they would prioritise exercise over other things. The people who always make time to exercise, no matter what else is going on in life, have exercise high up there in their hierarchy of values; they highly value it.

Before I knew about values, I used to say that money was important to me and I wanted to make lots of it... How very aspirational of me! Don't get me wrong, I did want to make money. Who doesn't? But the behaviour I carried out did not reflect the words I said, and behaviour is the most important thing. I was very good at talking about things like I meant them, but actions speak louder than words. The minute something more appealing, more important than making money, came up, I was off. Talking the talk is not the same as walking the walk!

Whether it's money, exercise, study, travel or anything else for that matter, being high up on the list of values is neither good nor bad; it's only an issue when you want something but that very thing is not important to you at the unconscious level. When the thought of actually taking action to do the thing you want to do doesn't make you want to get out of bed in the morning and you're not motivated to find time for it, regardless of whatever else is going on in life – and there will always be other things going on in life – then it can be a problem.

Values also form our moral compass and what we use to judge the difference between right and wrong. If someone acts in a way that violates our values, then we will feel negative emotions. They are there as a guide for us to know and enforce our own personal boundaries, and without them we wouldn't know what is deemed acceptable or not. For example, if someone highly values thoughtfulness in a relationship and their partner behaves in a way that they see as being unthoughtful towards them, they will feel negative emotions. When this happens it's important to let the other person know that it's not okay and enforce your boundaries, or let it go. When people neither address it nor forget about it, the emotion remains and often grows stronger, bubbling away in the background like a saucepan about to boil over!

Whilst I've given a couple of examples, it's important to note that values aren't limited to exercise and making money; they span across all areas of life and everything we do. I'm talking relationships, health, fitness, career, personal development, marriage, sex, travel, life... The list goes on!

Values are high-level, ambiguous words, such as security, freedom, flexibility, fun, variety, respect, happiness, excitement, love, achievement and recognition, that encompass a whole lot of meaning within them. The reason a particular value is important and the meaning of the word itself will be different for each person. Honesty in relationships to one person may mean knowing about their partner's past, their plans for the future and where the relationship fits in with those plans. Someone else's representation of honesty may be that they express their feelings to each other openly and often. Every person is an individual and no two minds work in the same way.

Back to motivation and where it comes from. When we were growing up, we'd absorb the unconscious messages we were receiving, so even if the values of those surrounding us weren't verbalised as being important, the seeds will have been planted in our young brains as we observed behaviours and imprinted those values in our own minds.

Here's the thing: times change and we also change as people, so the values that were instilled back then are more than likely out of date, or they just simply don't work for us and our goals now, but the brain is still programmed to be motivated to fulfil those same things. It would be like using a satnav from when you were five years old and expecting it to get you to your destination today. You just wouldn't do it, because you'd accept there to be a high probability that the satnav would no longer be effective at getting you to your desired destination. Many of the roads will have changed; new roads will have been added and the chances you'll arrive in the time predicted are highly reduced, if you managed to get there at all.

The mind is just the same. The programming that was installed back when we first came into this world is not the latest version available to us and because we are all different, with different goals and dreams, with different experiences along the way, that initial programming isn't necessarily the best for us.

Whilst I am all for encouraging everyone to take full responsibility for their life and everything in it, we can't actually take full credit for our values, because they aren't really our own – we inherited them. What we can do is take full responsibility for what we do next. Moaning that something isn't working and doing nothing to change it is a good way to feel stuck whilst irritating yourself and others. This isn't me lecturing in any way. I was that person for a long time. It was when I got bored of the sound of my own voice and listening to all the reasons why life was rubbish that I knew something had to give.

Our values are not set in stone… hooray! If you don't like them or they are not going to get you where you want to go in life, then you can change them. Without taking action towards this, the values we develop during those early years can often stay in place for life. That is, unless we experience an emotional event along the way, which all of us will do at some point.

When these events occur, the emotions associated with them can be either good or bad and the significance of those emotions will be different for each person. This could include anything from failing an exam, losing a job, having a baby, getting married or even breaking a leg. It can even include events that don't affect us personally but that have emotion connected to them, such as 9/11, Covid-19 and the lockdowns, recessions and other local, national or even global events.

There aren't any rules about what these events must be and how much emotion must be felt in order for them to change our values. When they do change, the things that used to be important to you no longer are; your perception is altered and new things make their way up your values hierarchy. You only have to look at people who have recently had a baby as an example of how values in every area of life can change in an instant. The minute that little bundle of joy comes into the world, everything changes. All the things that used to be the most important things in the world become irrelevant; priorities change and the motivation to fulfil those old things just isn't there anymore. But without those emotional events or doing intervention work with a professional coach to purposefully make changes, many of our values have the potential to stay in place throughout our lives.

Your values reside in your unconscious mind, the submarine. So, if the submarine is programmed and motivated to go north and the things you want are facing south, then it will feel like you're rowing against the tide because, metaphorically, you are. The first step is to know which direction the submarine is pointing in.

I will say this again as it's why many people give up and revert back to their old, ingrained behaviours and the reason why their life isn't what they want it to be. Whilst you may not be responsible for the values that were passed down to you, you are responsible for what you choose to do next!

Just knowing that your values are the very things responsible for your motivation is empowering. You have to understand what isn't working in order to change it.

Time to get to know yourself a little better!

ACTIVATION POINT – Discovering Values

Decide which area is of most importance to you right now, the one that impacts on your life the most. The one that, if changed, would also have the biggest impact on all the other areas of life too. Some examples are career, relationship, business, spirituality, health and fitness, family and friends.

Before you begin this exercise, remember that values are ambiguous words and phrases that have very little detail, such as freedom, happiness, security, protection and love. Each person's values will mean something different to them.

The key to carrying out this exercise effectively and really tapping into your unconscious mind is to do it quickly, writing whatever comes to mind, and to keep writing until you have nothing left to write.

Get yourself a notepad and make a list of your answers to the following questions:

1. **What is important to you about [insert the area of importance, e.g. career]?**

   Keep writing your list of the words that come to mind until you can't think of anything else.

   Remember that these are not the things that you want, they are the things that are important to you right now, even if you don't like them or wish they weren't important.

   Once you have finished, ask yourself the following question:

2. **What else is important to you about [insert the same area as question #1]?**

   Go! Write whatever comes to mind. Once you have finished, ask yourself one more time.

3. **What else is important to you about [insert the same area as question #1]?**

Write anything that is left until you have listed everything that is important to you in that area.

You should have at least eight values on the list by now. If not, ask yourself again until you do. Some of the values may be different words but mean the same thing, e.g. 'stability' and 'being grounded'. In this case, you can group these words together.

4. **Rewrite the list in order of importance, starting from the most important value down to the least important.**

Again, do this quickly. Your values live in your unconscious mind, so any analysis is your conscious mind kicking in.

What do you do if you're unsure which is the most important (because they are all important, right!)?

Ask yourself, out of the ones where you can't decide which to put first, if I could only have one of them in my life, which would it be? Once you've chosen, move to the next value on the list and do the same thing. There will probably be some values that initially feel equally as important but there will always be one that just has the edge. Trust your unconscious mind and whatever you think the answer is, go with that.

By this point you will have a list of your values, your motivators, in the area you chose to focus on first. This list should give you a good indication as to why you are where you are and the results you have created.

I did this process when I left a very unhealthy, almost 10-year relationship, and it explained a lot! I had overcome so many obstacles to leave the relationship and in doing so, I thought that all my issues had disappeared and I was ready for the world of dating!

What I quickly realised was that whilst I may have broken through the barriers of leaving the relationship, the things I held of value were still very much driven by the experiences I had been through. I was attracting different faces in different places but the same patterns were presenting themselves to me. I had spent years not valuing myself and seeing myself as being less than other people, undeserving of having a loving relationship, and the men I started dating reflected that back to me. They appeared to feel the same way about me as I did about myself.

> *The world is a mirror reflecting back at you.*
> *You'll only find love to the extent you are willing to love yourself.*

The things that were important to me were all based on what I didn't want. Let me explain what I mean by that.

Our values motivate us, but the energy behind each of our values and the reasons they are important to us is one of the biggest causes of why the motivation does or doesn't last.

The energy and the motivation behind each of our values is either driven towards what is wanted, which is all about the good stuff we'll get from them, or away from what is not wanted – the things we want to avoid in life.

I remember when I first heard this, I thought that it was obvious that my motivation was towards all the good stuff. I didn't want any of those unwanted things in life, so surely they wouldn't motivate me.

Well, it turns out it's not quite that simple.

The very fact that I knew that I *didn't* want them was a good indication that I was pushing against something.

Motivation to Avoid Pain

The motivation to not have pain is driven by the avoidance of the very thing you don't want and it's not always obvious that it's happening. It's not about excitedly feeling inspired to run in the direction of your goals; it's about not feeling the pain of its opposite.

We have experiences that cause us to feel negative emotions, anything from a health scare, not having enough money, being hurt by someone, being made redundant. An event happens that causes us to feel a negative emotion in the moment that we don't want to experience again. The reason we feel a negative emotion in those instances is because the event or experience is something that goes against our values. If someone values security in their career and they are threatened with redundancy, this will more than likely bring negative feelings to the surface, because their values are no longer being met; they are under threat. That can be the motivation for that person to take action to avoid what they don't want to happen.

Not only that, those events also have the potential to change our values. In a previous relationship, my partner at the time cheated on me and the things I valued and felt driven to look for changed. Overnight, things such as honesty, trust and monogamy became very important to me – things that, previously, I hadn't given any thought to.

Here's the important part: the reason they became important to me was because I didn't want to experience the emotions that made them important again. The motivation behind me seeking those very things were driven by the anger, the sadness, the hurt I felt and the fear that I would be cheated on again in the future.

This was also true of my health on a smaller scale. I didn't like the way I looked and so I was motivated to exercise and eat healthily. Yes, of course I wanted to look and feel a certain way but the reason and drive behind it was because I didn't want to stay as I was; I wanted to get away from the body I didn't like.

Imagine you're walking through a tunnel. One end of the tunnel has light shining through it; it's bright and everything you want is in the light. The other end of the tunnel is dark, with all the things you know you don't want. Along the tunnel there are many other walkways, other tunnels that veer off in different directions.

When you begin your journey of making changes in your life, you have to start somewhere, and the dark end of the tunnel is where many people set out from. You have to know what you don't want and what isn't working to know what you do want so that you can do something about it and begin to make changes.

You're starting your journey from the place of knowing what you don't want in life, at the dark end of the tunnel, and it doesn't feel good, so you feel motivated to step backwards and distance yourself from it. You are motivated to avoid the things that live in the darkness. You begin taking more steps backwards each day to get further and further away from the dark end of the tunnel. The light behind you is shining through the tunnel and so with each step backwards, it begins to get brighter and brighter. Relief!

The motivation to avoid pain does have its benefits. There is a lot of energy behind it. It's something you really don't want in your life, so it's a powerful way to kick-start momentum to take action but there are two main reasons why it doesn't last.

Reason #1: The pain wears off!

You've survived! The very thing that motivated you in the first place is now a distant memory and so it doesn't feel so bad. The pain has worn off.

A little bit of discomfort is tolerable and so few people take action when things are okay. It's only when something is painful enough that there is then a reason to change it. Think of it like wearing shoes that are a little too tight. A couple of hours wearing them whilst sat down is not ideal but it is doable and so many people would be willing to put up with that level of pain. If those same shoes had to be worn on a 10-mile hike, then the motivation to change them would be totally different.

After two days of eating takeaways and drinking more wine than I care to share with you, it was painful. I was tired, bloated, sluggish; my head was foggy, I felt depressed, my trousers felt tight, I ached all over and everything generally felt like hard work. I felt like I had metaphorically, or even physically in this case, taken myself for a 10-mile hike in a pair of shoes that were two sizes too small. Roll forward five days, after eating healthily and exercising, and the bloating had deflated, my trousers didn't feel so tight and I'd caught up on my sleep, so I was far enough away from the problem, the very thing that kick-started the motivation to be healthy in the first place. The drive to continue exercising and eating well became less and less, until it would eventually wear off completely. It would start with *"just the one"* and *"I deserve a treat,"* which eventually spiralled into a weekend of taking it to the extreme. It was only then, after yet another Saturday and Sunday of eating junk food like it was going out of fashion, with the promise that *"I'll start again on Monday"*, that it would begin to feel painful enough again and so the motivation would kick back in!

Like everything in life, it's not limited to one area, because we tend to take ourselves with us. This is something that can often be witnessed in business when someone is driven to set up their own company to get away from a job, a salary or a boss they don't want. When starting out in a new company, money may be in short supply and so the new business owner buckles up and does what they need to do to bring sales in. When things are tight and not going well, or how you want them to, there are a lot of reasons to knuckle down and get stuff done. They are avoiding the pain of not feeling secure, of not having enough money to pay the bills to keep a roof over their head and eat. They may want to avoid being in a position where they are not respected or they don't feel free, all the things that caused them to want to start the business to begin with. They work hard to make sure all those things don't come to fruition. The frustration, the fear, the hurt that led to their decision to set up on their own in the first place keeps them going. They take action consistently; they work hard and eventually they get results and there is money in the bank; the sales targets have been met; they can pay the bills and maybe even splash out a little.

Phew, relief!

They are out of the danger zone; they have successfully avoided the things they didn't want and so they take a breath and ease their foot off the gas and relax for a while. They can afford to – there's enough money to keep them going and they have worked hard so they deserve a rest. They have the day off, treat themselves to something new and shiny and enjoy the rewards of their labour. After some time has passed, the positive results they had been getting start to dwindle again. They stopped doing the very thing that caused them to achieve the sales, the activities that brought the money into the business in the first place, and so they dry up and so does the money. For every effect, there is something that caused it. In this case, the work they were doing caused the sales and when the work slowed down or stopped, so did the sales that followed. Eventually it becomes painful enough again. The money is running out and so the motivation kicks in and they get that booty into action. It's the boom-and-bust cycle and unless something changes, it can be one that repeats itself time and time again, over a whole lifetime.

You're back in the tunnel, stood near to and facing the dark end of it with the light shining behind you. You begin to move away from the dark end, taking step after step after step, getting further and further away. With each step you take, it becomes less dark and so the tunnel doesn't seem that bad now. It's easier to see around you

*now the light is closer so you can relax and stop for a break; walking
backwards is hard work after all.*

*Walking forwards is how you are designed and it's what you
normally do. It feels far easier to do; it's comfortable. For now, you
just take just a few steps forwards, back in the direction of the dark
end. You're just giving yourself a little break and you know that a
couple of steps won't make much of a difference in the grand scheme
of things. You definitely don't want to be in the dark end but you've
worked hard this week, so what's another couple of small steps? They
won't hurt. Before you know it, one step at a time has slowly but
surely taken you back into the tunnel, right back to the dark end.*

*It does not feel good there. In fact, you know full well that you really
don't want to be anywhere near there again and it's enough to make
you jump backwards and begin taking steps backwards again, away
from the dark end.*

It's a never-ending cycle of going backwards and forwards like
a yo-yo, without making much movement either way. This
inconsistency takes a lot of mental, physical and emotional energy
and usually doesn't take you to where you really want to go.

Reason #2: It has no direction!

When something is painful or unwanted in your life, the focus is
on being anywhere but there. In that moment, it doesn't matter
where you are going as long as it gets you away from the place you
don't want to be.

When I first started dating after 10 years of being off the market, it was so important to me that I found someone who I felt secure with because I didn't want to get hurt again. I looked for people who I believed would be honest because I was scared I was going to be lied to. I was motivated to find someone who wouldn't do the things that I didn't want or treat me in a way I didn't like, and I was happy to consider anyone who didn't display those traits or behave in those ways. The problem was that I wasn't taking steps to look for what I actually wanted in a relationship, because the truth was, I had no idea. My time was spent making sure that men didn't meet the criteria of unwanted things, without giving much time and thought, if any, to deciding where I was headed to next.

Think of it a bit like being close to a fire that is too hot. Who cares where you end up, as long as you don't get burnt! This can be a good thing at first because it stops you from feeling the heat from the fire so it's less painful. Here's the problem: the desire to avoid something is directionless. You're not heading towards anywhere; you're just moving away from somewhere without a place to go in mind. It becomes about surviving the heat, so anywhere is good as long as it's not hot anymore. When you begin to cool off, you may find that you don't like where you've ended up.

When you jump in your car and pull out your satnav, you have to input the destination you want to go to. Asking your satnav to take you away from where you currently are doesn't work. It doesn't know where it is going. Your mind works in just the same way.

Although you will begin to move away from the thing you don't want, your focus is still on it. Remember that you get what you focus on, whether you want it or not. Without choosing where you want to end up, the satnav is programmed to point in the direction of where you currently are and so you keep ending up back there.

You're back in the tunnel. The dark end is right in front of you. You're stood right in it and the light is shining behind you. You begin to move away from the dark end, taking step after step after step, getting further and further away, until you look around and wonder where you are. The light isn't behind you anymore. What happened?

Without a direction to head towards, you found yourself going off down one of the side tunnels. It wasn't necessarily where you wanted to go; you just knew you didn't want to be at the dark end of the tunnel. You have no idea where you are going because you're still walking backwards. You're using all your energy getting away from the dark end and you haven't taken the time to turn around and decide where to go next.

After a while, going backwards to nowhere gets tiring. How can you possibly stay motivated when you don't even know where you're heading? All you can think about is the dark end because you're looking right at it. All the walking backwards is feeling more like hard work and the dark end is so far away now. What does it matter if you have a rest? In fact, you're fed up of heading nowhere and a couple of steps forwards won't make much difference. It feels comfortable; it's easy to walk forwards. Step by step, day by day, before you know it, yet again, you end up back where you started!

When you unconsciously make the decision to avoid something, your energy is used to doing just that. But even when you're far enough away from it that it's no longer painful, your attention is still on it.

> *"What you resist, persists!"*
> **Carl Jung**

When you're still pointing your attention and focus in the direction of what you don't want, without realising it, as the motivation gradually off, you begin to make your way back towards it until it gets too painful again and the motivation kicks in… again. A life of what you are NOT going to do leads to self-sabotage because you get what you focus on.

Motivation to Thrive

Turning your attention towards having the motivation to thrive is where it's at. This type of motivation has direction. It's focused on and driven towards the things that you want.

When I made the decision to deal with the past baggage I had been carrying around from my previous relationship, I was surprised and delighted by the things that then became important to me and how my focus changed.

When the hurt, fear, anger, sadness, guilt and all the beliefs I held about myself and my worth were resolved, the values I had once had around honesty, respect, monogamy and so on all changed. My values became such wonderful things that had previously been out of my awareness. I valued love, happiness, fun, laughter, connection, and these values were all driven towards the pure desire to enjoy them. I was no longer running from the things I felt were lacking in my life or things I was worried would happen if I didn't have certain things present.

To give you just one example, trust in relationships was always high up in the things I valued in the past and it was because I didn't want someone I couldn't trust – there was negative emotion driving it. I had experienced mistrust and was still wearing the scars. In fact, the scars hadn't healed; the emotional cuts were still raw and this was obvious in the choices I made and the way I approached potential relationships. I had my guard up because I was afraid I would be hurt again. It caused such inner turmoil for me because I wanted to find love and be happy but, at the same time, I didn't want to let my guard down. I had an internal conflict going on and that was how I behaved – like I had a split personality. Part of me wanted to find someone but the other part of me didn't. I was unconsciously protecting myself on some level. Talk about mixed messages!

When I did finally release the conflict and the emotion behind the values, trust was no longer important. I no longer had any reason to not trust; it became irrelevant. I felt like I was able to breathe again!

I fully appreciate that not everyone is in the position right now to work with a professional coach and deal with the past and the emotions that go with it. If you are, I would be more than happy to recommend some amazing coaches who have the tools to release inner conflicts, past negative emotions and beliefs quickly, some of whom I have trained personally. If you're not able to right now, or if it's not for you, that's okay too. You can certainly begin to make changes through completing the exercises in this book. Just adjusting the direction of your focus alone will have a big impact on where that takes you and the consistency needed to get there.

You're in the tunnel. The dark end is in front of you and the light is shining behind. You realise that walking backwards isn't getting you very far and worse than that, all you can see is the darkness; so you decide to take the time to work out what you want, where you want to go, and you turn around to face in the direction of it, towards the light. You see the whole tunnel light up in front of you and you focus on walking towards the light, towards the positive things you desire.

Now that the tunnel is lit up, you can see a winding pathway in front of you, leading you into the light. The dark end still exists but it's behind you. It no longer drives you anymore. You're grateful for the experiences you've had in the darkness because without them you wouldn't know there is light; it gave you clarity. The difference now is that your focus is ahead of you, in the light and you feel pulled towards it. It's no longer about looking at the dark in an effort to leave it behind; it's about the shiny future in front of you, the things that are to come that you know are yours and you deserve!

Time to turn that focus around!

ACTIVATION POINT – *Changing Direction*

You have your list of values from the previous activation point. If you haven't completed this yet, do that first before you continue with this exercise.

Go through your list of values one at a time and ask yourself the following questions, writing down your answers as you do:

1. **What positive things can I learn from the experiences I have had that made this value important to me? What can I learn that will help me in the future?**

   Do this for each value before carrying on.

   For example,

   > **Value:** *Honesty*

   > **Learning:** *It's okay to just go with the flow, I can trust in myself.*

   > **Value:** *Security*

   > **Learning:** *I can choose what actions I take, I'm in control of my life.*

2. **Going through each value again, with the new positive learnings you now have, and ask yourself:**

   If I knew this value was a given, that I just know it is taken care of, what would I really want?

   Write down everything that you want, even if you have no idea how you will get it.

   For example,

   > *Honesty – if I knew this was a given then I would want* **Fun**

> *Security – if I knew this was a given then I would want* **Freedom**

Pretending that you don't want something when you do, doesn't make the desire go away. Be honest with yourself and enjoy it!

This is about deciding how you want your life to be so it should light you up when you think about it.

Once you've done this, it's time to check your focus.

3. **Re-read the things you have just written about, the things you want. Check if there is anything in there that is focused on not having something you don't want.**

The giveaways and words to look out for are…

"I won't…"

"I no longer…"

"I don't…"

"I haven't…"

"I'm not…"

"I have less…"

"I have enough…" This is a sneaky one. Having enough of something is based on lack and scarcity – it just about covers things. Rather than 'enough', what do you actually want?

4. Notice where your focus and attention go when you read it. What picture comes to mind?

Any values that are driven by avoidance will be facing the dead end of the tunnel; these are the things you want to get away from. Even if the image of what you don't want only flickers into your mind for a moment, it's still there.

Flip it by asking, what is the opposite of it?

The drive to thrive feels good! It feels expansive and energising. The feeling of avoiding pain is not energising; it feels draining and restrictive. Become familiar with the difference you feel internally between the two. This is feedback for what is going on unconsciously in the submarine of your mind, even when your conscious mind in the rowing boat isn't sure if it's heading in the right direction or not.

There are many ways to take a deeper dive into what is going on in the depths of your mind and I encourage you to do that whenever possible.

Your external world is filtered through your unconscious mind, which is the home of your beliefs, emotions, memories, view of energy, time, values, personality type and a number of other factors. When you make changes at the unconscious level, when you release the negative emotions and limiting beliefs that drive your motivation, you are essentially changing the lens that you see the world through and so the world you see changes. Your internal filters change, which automatically adjusts the things you delete, distort and generalise from your experience. The outside world is a mirror of your internal world and when one changes, the other is altered too. For physical manifestation to take place outside of you, the change to get there must happen inside first.

Tuning into and listening to yourself, getting to know what those unconscious filters are, is a great starting point and something you can do straightaway today.

Chapter 8
Failure Is Your Biggest Friend

"Failure is a greater teacher than success."
Clarissa Pinkola Estés

Getting things "wrong" is the quickest way to success!

I remember listening to an interview with the founder of Spanx, Sara Blakely, who said that every evening after school her dad would ask her what she had failed at that day. When I first heard this, I thought it was a very bizarre concept but when I began to really understand failure, it made total sense.

The easiest way to not fail is to not do anything, to not push yourself, to not do the things you don't already know, to not go outside of what's comfortable, to not do anything you feel uncertain about.

It's also the quickest way to not achieve anything in life!

Think back to the first time you tried tying your shoelaces. I imagine you probably weren't successful and if you did manage to get the laces to stay together, you probably didn't achieve the perfect bow. At that age, you also probably didn't apply any meaning to the experience, whether you managed to tie the shoelaces or not. We know that not being able to tie shoelaces doesn't mean that person is a complete failure. Just like not coming first in the egg-and-spoon race on sports day doesn't mean that child will never achieve anything when they grow up, and failing a maths exam doesn't mean that person will never make any money. Of course it doesn't! Failing at one thing does not mean anything. Whilst this is understood logically, when it comes to taking action towards our goals as adults, that logic seems to get lost.

Not getting things right first time can be frustrating; even at a young age we want to get that shoelace tied on the very first attempt. The difference at that age is that we expect to mess up and fail and we also know that even when we do, we are still loved; we are still enough. It doesn't define who we are. At some point during our transition from childhood to adulthood, getting things wrong begins to have meaning applied to it and that meaning is usually something that is not actually related to the failure itself.

Setting up a new business and not getting sales in the first month of trading does not mean the business won't work and that business owner will never be successful. Going on dates with six potential partners and not meeting someone suitable for a second date does not mean that individual is unlovable and destined to be alone forever. Eating too much chocolate on a Saturday night does not mean a person's diet is totally ruined and they will always be overweight.

The same principle applies in reverse too. Setting up a business and only working on it for a month does not make a successful business. Going on a date once does not make a loving relationship. Eating healthily one night a week is not how you lose weight. If you followed these guidelines, you would probably expect to fail.

Even though the concept of failure is understood, so many people will actively avoid it to the point they don't pursue the things they want.

Why is failure something that is feared?

I remember being in my early thirties and applying to be the lead singer in a band. It wasn't something I'd ever wanted to do before but I thought it would be good fun and a nice addition to the acting and modelling work I was doing at the time. The funny thing was that I had no real singing experience. I hadn't had any singing lessons and wasn't really sure if I sounded any good. All I knew was that I loved karaoke and I had received many compliments over the years, although it was coming from people who had usually had a lot to drink so their judgement probably wasn't a useful gauge of whether or not I had any real talent. When I applied for the audition, I didn't think I would actually get it, so I didn't give it much thought beyond the application...

... until the email landed in my inbox!

We would like to see you next Tuesday at 3pm for your audition. Please prepare x, y and z song.

I was invited to sing three different songs that included a mixture of range and styles, so they would be able to hear my vocal ability and see how I performed. I remember that one of the songs was a big number by Mariah Carey, something that would stretch even those with the best voice. Whilst I was able to use the mindset tools I had learnt to clear up any limiting beliefs about myself and give me the confidence I needed, I also knew that believing I had a voice that matched some of the world's greatest didn't mean that I actually did. Just like believing I am an amazing driver doesn't make me Lewis Hamilton. There would need to be some practised skill thrown into the mix too. Working only on the mental plane of existence doesn't magic things into the physical plane.

On the afternoon of the audition, I practised the songs I was going to sing. I visualised myself having completed them and being really pleased with my performance as the people auditioning me said how great I was. I was having such fun doing it, singing into my hairbrush like a diva, throwing around some dance moves and thinking I was the next Lady Gaga, when I suddenly found myself thinking about the fact that I may not get it. I could fail. Then what? What would that mean?

I started questioning myself. Who was I to audition? I had no experience. I was a fraud! If I went for it and didn't get it, that would just prove to me that I wasn't good enough and I didn't have what it takes. Any positive beliefs I had could be shattered if someone who knew more than I did told me I didn't have the talent, the look, the X factor. I suddenly felt scared!

The interesting thing is that in those few seconds nothing had actually changed in the world, yet I went from having fun and feeling excited to not having fun and feeling fearful in an instant. The experience I was having in that moment and the experience I would continue to have if I carried on feeling that way were completely altered by the meaning I had applied to it – me not being accepted into the band would mean I have no talent and I'm not good enough.

I very quickly found myself coming up with all sorts of reasons and excuses as to why I probably shouldn't bother going for the audition, finding problems that didn't even exist to rationalise my thinking. I decided that I may not be able to work on all the dates they want, I'm not sure that I like all of the songs they play; I'd probably end up having to work most Saturday nights and I don't think I want to do that; I don't know the other people in the band and we may not get on; maybe I shouldn't bother after all. I worked my way through at least 15 excuses to not go for it in the space of 30 seconds.

Then I sat with it for a few minutes to think about what was really going on.

I very quickly realised that, up to that point, all I'd really done was think about being in a band as something that I might do one day, which was fun. There was no pressure involved because it wasn't really happening, so I couldn't fail. Whereas the thought of actually putting myself in the position where I would actually be doing it – I would be singing in front of people and they would be judging me on my performance and deciding if I was good enough to join them or not – well, that was something different entirely. Beyond that, I could be performing in front of crowds of people who may not like what I have to offer. It meant that failing was possible!

My logic was that if I didn't do it, then I wouldn't fail. I could create reasons and excuses as to why I didn't pursue it in the first place and tell myself that was the reason it didn't happen, not because I failed. I couldn't fail at something that I didn't even try, which certainly felt like the safer option, the way to protect myself. By not putting myself in the position where I could be rejected, I wouldn't be. If I didn't do it, I wouldn't fail. But it also meant that I wouldn't succeed. Not succeeding because I didn't go for it would actually be the biggest failure of all.

Embracing Failure

I personally choose the belief that failure doesn't exist. In my world, not achieving something I set out to do is feedback so I can adapt and do it differently in the future. For the purposes of this section, I'm going to use the word 'failure' so you know what I'm referring to and how you can reframe and use it to benefit you.

Our unconscious mind is designed to protect us and so if it perceives something as a threat, it will look for ways to prevent it from happening. When we see not being successful at something as failure, our unconscious mind kicks in to keep us safe; it's doing its job. The problem is that whilst the intention is good, the result isn't always positive.

To stop this from happening, you need to get your unconscious mind on board so that it knows you are safe and no longer feels the need to step in when you think things may not work out. To do that, you need to reframe what failure means to you. It's time to break down the reality of failing!

Failure is quite simply a Future Attempt In Learning Until Reality Exists.

You are attempting to do something that will be a reality in the future, right now, which will cause you to learn in the process. Once you have done it, that very thing becomes your reality.

You can spend all day every day learning the theory of something; you can become the world's most versed in your knowledge about the subject but no amount of knowledge will outweigh what you will gain through the experience of it. You can read about swimming and how to do it; you can watch videos on it, learn about all the different strokes, how to have the best form, make yourself go faster, yet the only way to really know it is to do it. Even with all of the knowledge about it, you'll probably never feel ready to actually go and do it in practice. Knowing and doing are very different things. Jumping in the pool is the only real way you will learn to swim and, of course, no matter how much theory you know about swimming you wouldn't expect to get it right on your first attempt, which is why armbands and floats were invented.

Better to make mistakes, say and do things that don't work, instead of waiting until you have it all figured out. Even if it doesn't work, you'll learn along the way, until eventually something does.

I should mention that even when you know this stuff, you're still human and there will always be those unconscious patterns that need breaking to propel you forward, so it's better to get used to it and see the opportunity to grow than to wish away what could make for an interesting ride.

It's easy to put something off until you believe it's perfect or you are ready, but the reality is that you will never feel ready to do something for the first time. How can you be ready to do something you don't know? The quickest and the only way to become ready is to do it, just get started from wherever you are and work it out as you go. Fear of getting it wrong is usually what stops people from even beginning, and it's almost always about other people. Fear of what they will think, what they will say, how they will judge you if it doesn't work out as planned. If someone wants to criticise you for doing the things they are not doing, that is about them, not you. The world is a mirror reflecting back to you who you are, and if others take it upon themselves to notice the action you are taking with negativity, it's really a reflection of what they don't believe is possible or they are not doing for themselves. When this happens, send them love and then choose who you spend your time with. Having a supportive environment is fundamental to your growth as it's the foundation of everything you do.

Going back to the example of tying your shoelaces… You know that a child has to get it wrong so that they understand how to do it right and the same goes for everything else, even as an adult. When you begin to see taking action as an attempt to learn something that will be your reality in the future, the pressure is off, as there is no expectation you will know how to do it straightaway. Every time you take action, see it as practice, an opportunity to learn and improve, because the reality is that it is just that and it always will be. No matter how great you become at the things you desire, there is always more – it's a never-ending journey of growth and improvement.

Imagine if the Beatles sat back after creating their first album and never did anything different. They could've quite easily thought the music they knew and had already created worked and so there was nothing to change. Think of all the amazing songs we would've missed out on if they hadn't risked doing something that was unknown to them, unknown to the world. It goes without saying that some of the songs they wrote worked better than others in terms of their success. This didn't mean they failed; they just found ways that didn't work so well and they used that information to write their next songs differently.

Along with the Beatles, Sara Blakley's dad appeared to be a wise man. By encouraging Sara to fail at something every day, she had to go out and make mistakes. The quickest way to do that is by going into the unknown and doing the very things you don't know how to, the ones you are usually avoiding, which you are more likely to fail at. By pushing yourself to fail, you let your unconscious mind know that it's okay to fail. It's safe. In fact, you are looking for ways to do it because it's positive. If you do the very thing that you failed at again and again, taking on the feedback about what to do differently next time or what to work on, then each time you do it in the future, the chances of failing become less until success becomes the reality.

The more you fail, the less impact each failure has. It's then no longer the big thing that we so often turn it into, because if it doesn't work, it can be done again. Hardly anyone is successful on their first go and if everyone was successful at everything first time, then the world would be a pretty boring place as there would be nothing to strive for. The real joy of achievement is in the pursuit of it. When you arrive, you are there and so it's the new normal and there becomes a new aim, something else that you want and will probably not achieve when you first start out. Accept that no matter how far you go, there will always be failure because there is always something more to achieve.

Letting Go of Success

To let go of failure, you must also let go of success. When you hold on so tightly to what success must look like, you close off your mind to all the possible ways to achieve it.

A problem that often presents itself in the pursuit of a particular outcome is when you need it as opposed to want it. When you need something, when you are desperate for it, you repel it. You only have to think of the person who is desperate for a partner and ends up putting off any suiters that come their way. The saying 'you can smell the desperation' is really about the energy that person is radiating. Just like when you are in the presence of someone who is high vibe or low vibe and you feel it, desperation has its own energy.

To manifest something you want, you have to also be okay with not having it.

This may sound contradictory but the energy behind it makes all the difference. If the achievement of a particular outcome is held so tightly in an attempt to force it, it doesn't work and it prevents anything else making its way in. If you really want something to the point that you want it too much, your mindset may well be driven by the lack of it. Your focus becomes fixed on it being a certain way, to the exclusion of anything else, and you end up missing the various other ways it could come into your existence. It repels rather than attracts.

This is important: when your attention is fixed on the outcome being one way, you unconsciously reject everything outside of what you desire, anything that is not that thing you want. The problem is that anything you reject or don't want must be in your awareness. By having the frame of mind that something *must* happen, you notice everything that is not that, in other words, what you don't want. Your unconscious mind is focused on and draws your attention to the many ways to create those very things. My audition for the band was one way of achieving my goal to sing for fun outside of just doing a karaoke, and I could quite easily fail. Failure in this instance being that I may not be accepted into that particular band, and there was a good chance of that happening. If I'd needed that audition to be successful and decided this was my only shot, it would've shifted my internal reality – the feelings I had about it, the images it created in my mind and how I turned up and performed. It makes the thing you want the answer and the truth is that the answer is already inside you and there are many ways to create the physical representation in your external world.

Keeping focused whilst having flexibility is one way to stay open. Your focus activates your RAS and flexibility shows you all the other routes to the destination you desire. I have witnessed many people in my life who have applied for the job they say they really want and who, when not invited for an interview following their first application, gave up and resigned themselves to the fact they will never have the job they want, so there is no point even trying. They have gone on to spend their whole lives doing jobs they hate and moaning about the fact they weren't even given the chance to interview for the company they love. More often than not, they didn't even attempt a second go at an interview. They had all their eggs in one basket with a single route of getting there which, when not successful on the first attempt, they saw as failure because it didn't work out as planned.

The things you want can come in many forms, many ways that us mere humans in our own world haven't even considered. When you realise this, you will also see there really is no such thing as failure. If one way doesn't work, there will always be another that does.

I love the story of the drowning man and it's a great metaphor to take on board. In case you haven't heard it, here is a short synopsis:

> A man found himself trapped in his house after a flood made its way through the town where he lived. The man began praying to God to come and rescue him. As the water started to rise, his neighbour offered to help. He had a pick-up truck that was big enough to get them through the rising water and take them to safety. The man refused, telling his neighbour, *"I am waiting for God to save me."* And so his neighbour left him.
>
> The floods were getting worse and the water started rising even higher. The man had to make his way up to the roof of his house. He was continuing to pray to God to save him when a boat passed by. The people on the boat shouted to the man to join them to head to safety but again the man refused. He told them he was waiting for God to rescue him and so they carried on without him.

The man absolutely believed that God would come through and save him. He carried on praying as the water kept rising. A short while later, a helicopter flew by and the man heard a voice over a speaker, offering to throw him a ladder and take him to safety. Again, the man refused. He shouted to the voice from the helicopter that God was going to save him, and so the helicopter flew away, leaving the man on the roof. Eventually, the water became too high; it swept the man away and he drowned.

As he arrived at the gates of heaven, he came face to face with God. He asked God why he had not saved him. He had believed with every fibre of his being that God would rescue him but he had let him drown. God was confused by this question and told the man, *"I sent you a pick-up truck, a boat, and a helicopter and you turned all of them away. What else could I have done?"*

Keep in mind, 'this or something better' and always be open and flexible.

The trick is to make every failure count, turning it into a success!

Every time you experience a perceived failure, there is always something to learn, something you can improve upon next time. If you don't get the interview upon first application, how can you adapt your CV next time? Who else could you contact to connect with the company you love? What could you do that you haven't considered yet? What is it you love about that company that other companies may have? Which other companies offer the same things you love about that particular company? What is your purpose for wanting to achieve that outcome? The reason for doing it is so much bigger than the thing itself – that is just one way you can have it. Failure can be the most amazing gift to you if you choose to see it that way.

It was 2.45pm on Tuesday afternoon and I had arrived for my audition. I'd watched some YouTube videos about warming up my vocals beforehand, which I thought would be helpful but I actually found my voice was starting to feel quite tired and I hadn't even started yet – oops! I saw the person who was auditioning before me finishing off her last song, the big one, and oh my gosh, she was good.

At that moment I could've quite easily decided there was no point even bothering because her voice was so much better than mine. She had clearly done this before but during my reflection earlier that day I had worked out that I had no idea what the band were actually looking for. I had been briefed about what they wanted me to do and what the band was about but I didn't know what criteria they had in mind. That also meant that no matter what happened, I couldn't fail. I may be the best singer in the world, with amazing dance moves, but if they are looking for someone who looks a certain way, has a particular tone of voice, a vibe about them that I don't fit, then I probably won't be the one they choose. This doesn't mean I'm not good enough or not worthy or a failure; it just means this isn't the one for me right now and I can learn from the experience.

It came time for me to step up to the stage. There was a video camera pointing at me; the band was to the side ready to play. I'd never played with a live band, by the way, and there were two other band members sat in front of me, ready to judge. They told me which song to start with and the band counted me in.

From that point on, it was a bit of blur. All I know is that I decided I would just completely enjoy myself and be totally me. Putting on a performance that was anything less than who I really was would be exhausting and very short-lived. I know there were times when my voice squeaked in places it shouldn't. I didn't hit the high notes in parts and I completely forgot the words during one song but I made some up in their place. It was as if I'd had my very own karaoke night with a live band. I had the most fun ever and said my goodbyes, thanking them for giving me the opportunity to sing.

The following day, I received a call from the band members to let me know how I had got on. The verdict: I had failed! I wasn't accepted into the band. That's how I could've looked at it anyway. What they actually said was that my energy and enthusiasm was intoxicating and my performance was brilliant. They also said that they do have a few bigger songs they play regularly and my vocals just didn't seem up to it. They had concerns about how I would manage playing a 45-minute set. I really appreciated their feedback and agreed that I would struggle. I would've most likely lost my voice before the set had finished. I hadn't become the person I needed to be for that position and that was okay.

There really is no such thing as failure. There is always an opportunity to evaluate and learn from everything you do. It's easy to use experiences that didn't work out as planned as the reason to not keep going, maybe even blaming others for not having successfully achieved what you want, but that just guarantees staying stuck.

The other option is to take those experiences and decide what you will do differently next time, looking at how you can improve or adapt so that the same mistakes aren't made. I decided to book myself in for singing lessons because I knew my voice didn't have the power to continually sing for 45 minutes without becoming croaky. This helped me massively and I did go on to sing a number of times in front of an audience, with my very own slot, and I enjoyed every second of it!

Success is how you choose to respond to and look at the inevitable failures. It is the very best way to grow because without it there is no feedback to improve upon. When you begin to see every failure as a way to propel yourself forward on your journey to success, failure truly becomes your best friend.

The biggest failures bring the biggest opportunities!

ACTIVATION POINT – Failing Big

Time to go and fail (or should I say learn?)!

Answer the following questions:

- **What have I been avoiding through the fear I will fail?**

  List all the things you want to do that you don't want to get wrong or mess up.

- **What would happen if I did fail?**

  Get it out of your head! What is the worst-case scenario?

- **If that happened, then what?**

  If the worst-case scenario was a reality, what would happen?

  How would you handle it?

- **What are the positive things that could come from failing?**

  How would doing it, regardless of whether it worked or not, improve your life?

Putting it into practice

If you knew you could never fail, what would you do differently?

- **Go and do it!**

  Aim to fail at least once a day and learn from it.

  After every go, ask yourself the following questions:

- **What did I learn from it?**

  Make sure the things you learn are positive. This isn't about criticising yourself; it's about looking at what worked, what didn't work and how knowing that information will benefit you to do better in the future.

- **What will I do differently next time?**

  Take what you have learnt and decide how you will adapt and change what you do next time, knowing what you now know.

Chapter 9
Ready, Steady, Action

"You don't have to be great to start,
but you have to start to be great."
Zig Ziglar

The magical word that makes all the difference, the word that is a must, is also the one that often gets lost along the way... ACTION!

This was the biggest mistake that I made when I discovered we are in control of our own realities. When I heard the word 'attraction', I just assumed I could sit at home and attract things to me without any effort on my part. If you think about the word 'attraction', no matter what context you use it in, there must be an input from the person doing the attracting. In the world of relationships, to attract a partner, you have to show up – you have to be out there for them to know you exist. It's the same with a job, money, clients and everything else in life.

Attraction is a two-way street!

Think of attraction like a magnet pulling itself towards all the things that are a match. Everything you desire has a frequency and when your energy vibrates at the same frequency as those things for a sustained period of time, they are pulled towards you. This is again why the intensity of your feelings matter: the more intense the feeling, the more pull there is; the less intense the feeling, the less the pull. And the more pull, the faster the time to creation.

When you have a thought of having something and you practice the feeling of having it, you are drawing it to you, which means you have the possibility of bringing it into your physical reality. If there is then no action taken towards it, you're giving mixed messages to your unconscious mind. Using the creation of a relationship as an example, if you declare that you want a relationship, you think about it, picture it, feel it and believe it will happen and then you sit at home every day never interacting with anyone else in real life, or even online, then you probably won't meet the love of your life. Short of the delivery driver or door-to-door salesperson being the match you are looking for, you're not putting yourself in the position to meet with the opportunities that are lined up for you.

When this happens, the message that you want a relationship and the action you take towards meeting someone are contradicting each other. This can lead to internal conflicts and mixed messages in the energy you emit.

"I want it but…"

"… I'm not going out to meet someone."

"… it's not important enough for me to do anything about."

"… I'm not invested in achieving it."

"… I don't really believe it will happen so there's no point trying."

Whilst you may not be consciously thinking these things, at an unconscious level, there will be something that is not in alignment with the things you say you want, therefore the frequency you vibrate at is not a match. It may be that sometimes you believe it but not other times and so it creates a pulling towards and then a pushing away from the things you want. This may well appear as mixed messages in the way you behave with others because you are giving out different frequencies at different times. Those mixed frequencies are what stops the physical manifestations coming into your life. As soon as your manifestations are nearby and ready to come into physical form, they get pushed back again and stay in the energy realm as a possibility.

Taking action shows your unconscious mind that you mean business. You're willing to play your part in the creation of the things you want, stepping into the possibilities that come your way to make them probabilities and then reality. Just think about how this takes place in day-to-day life as a metaphor: if you were to decide you wanted a certain body shape or size or you wanted your garden to look a certain way, or you wanted to travel to a certain destination, you know that in all of these scenarios you would absolutely have to take action for it to be achieved. You would need to eat certain foods and exercise, do some digging, buy plants, mow the lawn, book a flight and find accommodation; they all require action. Not a single one of them will magically appear in your lap whilst you're sat meditating. You have declared that you want those things and set the intention to achieve them. They are done in the quantum world of possibility. Your job is to focus on them and feel good about at least 51% of the time, even when the day-to-day of life throws itself at you, continually increasing that percentage of time and focus as you become more aligned every day. When you are able to focus on the reality you want more than you focus on your reality as it currently stands, the things you desire will come to meet you with ease. And to do that, you need to be there and ready to receive them. The life you are living right now is a manifestation of focus, the thoughts, beliefs, feelings and expectations you have had up to this point, and that can be changed if it's not what you want!

Activation of Action

What action should I take and when?

Taking action isn't about having all the answers and the truth is you won't have them all; it's about getting started. Imagine all the possibilities that could happen, all the ways you could receive the things you want. You couldn't possibly know what they are, so trying to plan the exact route to get where you want to go never works.

When you put your destination into your satnav, you fully expect and trust that you will arrive at where you want to go. You may not know the entire route, just where you are starting and where you will end up. You also know there may be roadworks, diversions, traffic and any number of things that may take you off the intended track at times. This doesn't stop you from doing it anyway, knowing you'll eventually get there. Imagine how long it would take to get anywhere if you waited until you knew all the details of the journey you were taking before you left the house. If you had to look up each and every turn you were taking along the way, every pothole you may bump across, all the cars and people you could interact with. By the time you had the full plan ready to go, things will have changed and you'd have to go back to square one to plan the whole journey again.

It may sound ridiculous to even think that way about jumping in your vehicle and going from A to B, yet this is what many people do when it comes to taking action in other areas of their lives. Rather than just keying in the destination of where they want to go – in other words, setting the goal and intention and then getting started without knowing all the turns and potential obstacles that will inevitably come up along the way – they wait until they think they have all the answers, which of course they never do. It's only when you start moving that the answers present themselves.

When you do begin taking action, your frequency changes because you are taking those steps towards the outcome you desire. This directs your focus and sends signals to your unconscious mind of what is important... ACTIVATE THE RAS!

Your reticular activating system is alerted and its focus changes, bringing to your attention the next step to take, the next road to go down, routes you may not have otherwise noticed.

If you want to start a business and you begin taking action to attract new clients, your RAS filters out all of the irrelevant information and homes in on the answers that will lead you there. Whether that is the best marketing platform for you, the social media post you write that connects you with your potential clients, the person who can help you with exactly what you need. All these things are able to enter through the gateway of your unconscious mind and be brought to the attention of your conscious mind. When they are brought into your awareness, they'll feel good because the frequency is a match with your outcomes and so you'll feel inspired.

When you feel inspired to take action, you are in alignment with the direction of your desires!

Inspired action isn't about getting busy doing things that feel hard. It's also not about everything being easy and not having to do the work. The universal Law of Cause and Effect states that for every effect, for everything that happens, there will have been a cause that preceded it. Applying this law to action means you can more accurately predict the chances of your success based on the input required to achieve the output desired and vice versa.

This consists of the mental and emotional factors – the thoughts we have, the internal conversations, the things that are important to us, the beliefs we hold to be true or not and the way we feel. Then there is our behaviour, the action that we take.

Taking action you feel rubbish about or believe won't work is like running in sand – it's hard work and you don't get anywhere quickly. It will feel like one step forward, two steps back and this will be evident in your energy too. We've all known of someone, or even been that person ourselves, who makes you wonder why they are even bothering to do something, as all they do is moan about it or their heart clearly isn't in it.

You know when someone says they are fine but the feeling you get from them is the total opposite of fine? That is the energy and the message that is emitted when action is taken from that place and it makes it a slow and painful process. The message of 'this is hard work' creates and attracts more hard work!

When someone is coming at it from this place, it's easy to appreciate why many people avoid taking action. A life that isn't enjoyable without the belief that there will be any reward at the end of it doesn't feel very inspiring.

Inspired Action

Take action and do the things you feel inspired to do.

Inspired action is when you have that idea, you feel compelled to do something, you wonder whether you should pick up the phone to that person, the same thought keeps coming to mind, it feels aligned even if it doesn't make sense right now.

As I sit here writing this chapter, it's 10.30pm on a Thursday evening. I've had a long week and I'm tired but I feel inspired to sit down and just get the words out. I wasn't even sure what those words would be but I knew that if I did what I felt inspired to do and write, they would come.

It would be so easy to think, *I'll wait until tomorrow after I've had a good night's sleep.* But I know unless I wake up really early, my diary is full and once the day begins, I'll be fully focused on that. I also know the inspiration may not be there in the same way that it is right now. It would also be easy to think, *It's been a long and busy week and I deserve to sit on the couch and relax with a glass of wine*, and most people would encourage me to do just that...

"Give yourself a break. You deserve it."

"You work hard. You need some time off."

"It's important that you get your rest."

"Do it at the weekend if you have an hour spare."

I'm sure many of these would be said with love and good intention. The problem is that goals require action and that will probably feel uncomfortable at times. Whilst taking action may not be easy, it is often exactly what you need to do for the creation of what you desire to come to fruition.

There are varying scales of action. You may have heard this before and I've said it myself: you must take BIG ACTION! It usually is true that the bigger the action, the bigger the reaction, or result, you'll get. However, big action can sometimes lead to the creation of negative emotions. Someone quitting their job today to dive into their new business that they have barely even started could create big problems when it comes to the end of the month and they have no money to keep a roof over their head and food on the table. If they don't have the finances to support the essentials to live, then their belief system will be put to the test and more than likely fall short if it hasn't the strength or evidence to support them in knowing they can do it.

I personally believe that action is about taking consistent steps every day, which lead to big results. I could sit here all night and write 30 pages of this book but if that's all I do for six months, I won't get very far, whereas writing a page every day for six months will very quickly add up. It also creates the habit of doing it, so on those days where it would be easy to not bother, the mental muscle has been flexed enough times that it can do it more easily, plus there is momentum. My RAS notices the times and opportunities to fit in writing the book. It also makes me aware of the experiences that happen throughout my day, which I then feel inspired to write about. My RAS provides me with the content I am looking for.

With each step you take, you are tipping the scales in your favour, even if it doesn't feel like it at the time. Those incremental steps taken day by day, over time, add up to big dreams, and the good part is that it is something we can all begin doing straightaway!

Chapter 10
Stepping into the Unknown

*"The journey of a thousand miles
begins with one step."*
Lao Tzu

❝*I* don't know HOW to get there.*"
The biggest stumbling block I had for a long time – and from experience I know I'm not alone with this one – was how to create the life I wanted, how to achieve my goals. You know where you are and you know where you want to get to, but how do you get there?

It was like knowing my desired outcome was to bake and eat my very own cake (Who doesn't want to have their cake and eat it?), and then seeing perfectly made cakes everywhere but having no idea how the cake was made. If you've never baked a cake before and you don't have a recipe, where do you start? I couldn't get my head around the logistics of getting from A to B, working out how people knew what ingredients were needed, the quantities, the order you put them in, where you got them from in the first place, the temperature of the oven and how long to bake the cake for.

It got even more confusing when different people would say there were different ways to bake the same cake. Approaching cake baking with all of these unanswered questions can feel overwhelming, usually leading to mental paralysis and not taking any action. I knew that without action, there would be no cake… or anything else for that matter!

When you look at getting from A to B like I used to, it definitely puts you at a disadvantage, because the truth is you won't know how to bake a cake if you haven't done it before. If everyone knew how to do everything before they ever did it, then there would be nothing new to learn.

Dreaming with the Breaks On

When it comes to creating your dream life, you really shouldn't know how you're going to achieve it and if you do, then the chances are it isn't as big a dream as it could be. Goal setting is usually carried out within the limitations of a person's thinking. This includes the beliefs they have about themselves and what they are capable of and it's the reason that setting small goals is so common – it keeps people feeling safe. One of the biggest fears is the fear of failure and when you dream big, there is a higher probability that failure is possible.

Better to play it safe and achieve what you know is probable than to dream big and know you might not achieve it, right?

No!!!

Lowering the bar to achieve something you find easy never inspired anyone. In fact, it's one of the quickest ways to lose motivation. If the goals you set yourself are things you already know how to do and it's just a case of doing them, then you already know what you need to do. Doing something new may require you to seek help and support from others, gain new skills, find the right community, maybe even hire a coach to help change your thinking to stop procrastinating so you can do it.

When I say "dream big", I'm talking about those things you think about when you dare to go there. The ones that many don't even talk about because they are quite simply dreams.

By the way, it's okay for your dreams to be your own dreams and not what society generally deems as "big dreams". Not everyone wants to have their own jet, a yacht and private chef on their own island and, equally, if that is the dream, that's okay too. If we all wanted to have exactly the same life, then it would be a pretty boring world. Someone who loves cooking may prefer to do their own rather than hire a professional. We are all different and it is our differences that make us who we are. Be honest with yourself about what you really want to create in your life, because you'll never be motivated to achieve someone else's dreams.

Think about what the commitment is on your end to actualise the dream. Do you really want it or do you just like the thought of it?

Whilst being a professional athlete may sound appealing, are you ready and willing to do the training and follow the diet needed? Are you prepared to give up social events, wake up early, deal with injuries, not see your family, have the majority of your time totally focused on your sport?

The resistance to what comes with the goal will eventually play out and prevent you from achieving it. If the reality of having the dream isn't what you really want, it's better to be honest with yourself now, rather than find out later. Use the energy you have to create what YOU truly want for you.

Taking the First Step

You have your last step, the destination. You know where you are heading. The only thing you need to know right now, in this very moment, is the first step you will take to begin to move yourself towards it.

You may be thinking, *But what about all the steps in-between?*

It doesn't matter!

> *"It's not knowing what to do, it's doing what you know."*
> **Tony Robbins**

If your goal is to bake a cake and eat it, but you don't know how to get from start to finish, the first step could be to find a recipe. Only when you have found your recipe will you take the next step, which could be finding out where to buy the ingredients from to give you the cake you want. You could end up going straight to a supermarket that sells Chinese food rather than the sugar and icing you were looking for, so you take the feedback, you learn from the experience and next time you look at where to go before just turning up. Once you have sourced and purchased your ingredients, you're on to the next step. One step at a time.

Taking the first step is crucial for so many reasons. One being that you are showing the universe that you mean business. Saying you want something and then going on with life as usual isn't going to change anything. The goal sets the aim and activates your RAS. Your RAS is now on high alert to look for information that is important and relates to your goal. When you take the first step, your unconscious mind becomes even more focused. The messages you send to your unconscious mind that it's happening, you're doing it, you're making progress, you're taking a step, even if it's only a small step, it's still a step. Your RAS will begin searching for the next steps for you!

I used to think that if someone would just tell me what to do, then I'd go and do it. What I was really looking for was certainty in how it would happen. Certainty is really the avoidance of uncertainty, the unknown, and the unknown is viewed as a scary place for most people.

"You don't know what you're walking into."

"Better to be safe than sorry."

"Better the devil you know."

"At least you know what you're getting into."

Common phrases to make us feel better about not stepping outside of what's comfortable.

If I'd have carried on using that mindset, I would still be in a toxic relationship. I would've continued to think, *Yes, he was cheating; yes, he treated me badly but at least I knew what I was getting, so there were no surprises.* It felt terrible being there but I'd gotten used to feeling bad. I'd learnt to deal with it, or so I thought.

These beliefs are used as the reason to settle in life and avoid making a mistake and suffering because of it. Settling doesn't work, because you know you are destined for more, otherwise you wouldn't be reading this book right now. Allow yourself to dream big, knowing that if you can conceive it, then it can be yours.

ACTIVATION POINT – Stepping Forward

- **Take a moment to write down any phrases that you may have used yourself, either now or in the past to justify staying comfortable.**

  Go through each item on the list and ask yourself the following:

- **What is the belief I have about this?**

  For example,

  Statement: *Better to be safe than sorry.*

  Belief: *I'm worried I'll fail.*

Statement: *At least you know what you're getting.*

Belief: *I'm scared that I won't know what to do.*

Using the list of beliefs you now have, go through each one and ask yourself the following questions:

- **What would happen if it wasn't true?**
- **How many ways do I know that it's not true?**
- **When has it not been true?**

You will find yourself noticing all the ways that those beliefs aren't real, so you can choose to let them go if they are not serving you.

You can also use the activation point 'Bridging the Gap' in Chapter 5 to create your own stepping-stones to a new belief.

ACTION TIME!!

- **What is the very first step you will take towards your end goal?**

  Remember, you don't need to and shouldn't know all the steps in between; you just need to get the ball rolling, and your RAS will show you the way as the path begins to light up for you, one step at a time.

- **Go and do it now!**

  If you are able, take that first step right now. Do it immediately!

If it's not appropriate this very second, put a date and time in your diary for when you will do it, ideally within 48 hours. Commit to getting it done. Tell someone you love that you're doing it and ask them to check in with you to make sure you have.

Once you've done it, congratulate yourself. Give yourself some love. You've started! Celebrating the small wins creates a positive association with taking action. All you need to do after that is decide what the next step is.

One step at a time leads to big miracles!

Chapter 11
When the Going Gets Tough

When you have control of your mind,
you have control of everything.

It's now time to get real!

Putting everything you have learnt into practice is much easier to do when life is running smoothly and there's nothing out of the ordinary to deal with, but what about when adversity happens?

One thing you can guarantee in life is there will be a time when you will face some sort of adversity and whilst everyone's experience will vary in how hard those times may be, they will happen at some point. These hurdles are metaphorical forks in the road and you have the choice to go either way.

You can use them as the reason to give up or see them as an opportunity to test your commitment and keep going!

I'm personally going through my own testing time as I write this very chapter. In fact, it's the reason why I chose to include it and I also believe that may very well be the reason I'm experiencing it. I'm sure that giving a real-life account of how to put this stuff into action when life gets a little bumpy will be of immense value.

Every tragedy, every setback, every hardship we face doesn't have to just be about getting through it. It can also be used as a chance to evolve and come out the other side thriving.

In Chapter 2, we touched on the universal laws, one of those being the Law of Rhythm. All things rise and fall. For every up, there is a down; for every high, there is an equal low. The pendulum must swing in both directions in equal measure. When times are really tough, there has to be an equal positive that follows.

It's only fair that I share with you what I'm going through and how I use these practices every day to stay positive and come out the other end stronger.

I recently found a lump in my breast and the following day I was told I was being referred as a high-priority case to check if the lump is cancerous. Right now I'm in a state of limbo.

I'm not going to pretend that being an expert in all things mindset doesn't mean I never feel emotional. Negative emotions are there as feedback that something is going against our values. So if something is important to us and that very thing is being violated or not being met, then there will be emotion present to let us know.

When the doctor said I needed to see somebody soon, if I'm honest, I initially didn't feel anything. I went into what you could probably call survival mode and I just thought about all the practicalities. My diary was full for the next few weeks so I'd have to speak with my business partner about having a day off to go to the hospital. I had a training call that evening so my focus was completely diverted back to that. It wasn't until later that evening, after the call had finished, that I began to even think about what had been said in the doctor's surgery.

I didn't sleep well that night but I didn't think much either. I was just awake and my mind was blank. It was only when I got up the next morning that I began to feel emotional and I needed to cry. I let myself! Crying is a release of energy, which is why it can feel so good after a big old sob. When you feel like crying, do it. Holding tears back is like squeezing into a pair of trousers with a waistband that is too tight. When you loosen the waistband, you can breathe properly again, and it's the same with crying; you will feel better. Maybe a little tired at first but better for letting it out.

Next, I decided to write down my thoughts and feelings. Up until that point, I hadn't really had many, or I hadn't consciously acknowledged them, but once I started writing, they came flooding out. A great way to process what is going on internally is to just write without thinking. Allow your unconscious mind to take over and say whatever needs to be said —writing for yourself only, knowing that no one else will read it. When you write something thinking that someone else will see it, it influences the words you choose by how much you are willing to share and the opinion you think they may have, so do it just for you. If you're angry, write it down. If you're sad, write that. Getting it out of your head and onto paper helps to stop thoughts bouncing around non-stop. It's like a shopping list – until you have written it down, you hold the items you need in the back of your mind. When you put pen to paper, you can forget about them until you go shopping.

I'm not comparing a shopping list to the traumas that people experience in any way. What I do want to demonstrate is that aside from the emotions that go with it, the unconscious mind doesn't know the difference between a shopping list and thinking about how someone will survive financially or get through an illness when it comes to processing information. Either way, if it's out of your mind and on paper, some of that processing can stop, even if just for a short while.

After spending a good 30 minutes or so writing down everything I was thinking, even the things I didn't know I was thinking, I felt lighter. I had mentally emptied out and felt able to take a minute. It was only then that I reflected on what was going on and what came to mind may well sound bizarre to most.

I love understanding human behaviour so I couldn't help but consider how interesting the last 24 hours had been. 'Interesting' may sound like a bit of an odd word given the situation, so let me elaborate.

<u>Monday afternoon, the day of the lump finding.</u>

On Monday morning, the lump didn't exist in my reality and so I had no feelings about it.

<u>Monday evening, the finding of the lump.</u>

The lump now exists and I plan to get it checked to make sure I'm okay. No need for concern.

<u>Tuesday afternoon, the examination.</u>

The doctor feels the lump and also finds some hard tissue surrounding the outer area and lumps under the armpits. I'm referred as an urgent case to check if there is any cause for concern. I felt a little concerned.

In the 48-hour period, nothing has actually physically changed in my world, yet my perception has. Although short-lived, I did play through the 'what if' scenario and of course, this is a possibility. The interesting part of this is that at the moment, whilst I'm writing this and I'm waiting for my appointment, I neither have nor don't have breast cancer.

To give you some idea of what I mean by this, there's an experiment known as 'Schrödinger's cat', which was carried out in the imagination of a quantum physicist, Erwin Schrödinger. It didn't actually take place.

In this experiment, a cat was placed in a sealed box with a device that may or may not release radioactive poison within the next hour, which would of course kill the cat. The odds were 50:50. There was a 50% chance the device would go off and kill the cat and a 50% chance it wouldn't and the cat would live.

There are multiple realities going on and the cat is a blur of probability because until you open the box, the cat is both alive and dead at the same time. It's only the observation of something that makes it real. It takes the waves of possibility and collapses them into a particle through observation. Of course, when you look in the box, you will know if the cat is dead or alive, but up to that point, the cat is both dead and alive at the same time because both waves of possibility exist.

Coming back to the lump, I now know something that I didn't know before, i.e. there is a lump which may or may not be cancerous. I also know there are things that I don't know, i.e. whether or not the lump is cancerous. At this very moment in time I have multiple realities of possibility that exist, which means I also have a choice.

I could choose to focus on, observe and look at the one where I am diagnosed with cancer. That is one possibility. Another possibility is the one where I am told it is a cyst and I can go home a little more lumpy than I used to be. Both possibilities exist at the same time until I am told either way. When I wake up in the morning, it will be just another Thursday, no different to the one just gone. The only thing that would make it something other than that is my thinking about it. Until I see the specialist, I won't know what the outcome is, but the one I choose to focus on is the reality I will experience until that day.

Just like the cat, until the box is opened, the cat is both dead and alive but thinking about the cat being dead before you actually know will probably make your experience in that moment feel not so good.

The point of all of this is that, right now, I am living in a space of possibility in terms of knowing for sure what the lump is and I know the version of reality I choose to think about and focus on will be one of the biggest factors in how good or bad I feel today. I'm choosing to see myself and focus on having a glass of something fizzy to celebrate the doctor giving me the all-clear.

This isn't about putting my head in the sand, and I know I may wobble at times; it's about working with the things that are within my control. I cannot control how quickly my appointment comes through. I cannot control the news the doctor gives me but what I can control is where to purposefully place my attention between now and then. I can also make sure I look after myself physically to ensure I feel as good and positive as possible, making sure I get plenty of good, nutritious food, sleep, exercise, fresh air and water. The way you feel physically has a massive impact on the way you feel emotionally, so always look after both.

I truly believe there is always something to learn from everything that happens in life and that learning can be used to make positive changes in the future, changes we may not otherwise have had the opportunity to know about.

My learning so far: I can choose how to navigate my way through this period of the unknown. My thoughts and where I place them are my responsibility. If I feel emotional at times, that's okay; I'm human. How long I decide to stay wallowing is up to me. I will only ever be given the things I am able to handle, therefore I can get through anything that comes my way.

I have to be totally honest here and confess that lumps aren't something I check for as regularly as I probably should but it was something my mind told me to do.

Learning number two: when I get those hunches, those intuitions, trust myself! Intuition comes from your unconscious mind and your unconscious mind knows more than you may think, particularly when it comes to your body, so listen. Your unconscious mind knows the blueprint for perfect health, which is why it also knows when we have anything less than that. The number of times I have thought I should do something and then brushed it off, only to later find I was right.

ACTIVATION POINT – *Taking Control*

This particular activation is super useful when difficult times present themselves, which they inevitably will at some point.

- **Get everything out of your head and onto paper**

  Write down what you are feeling, thinking, saying to yourself. Get it all out, even the things you think you shouldn't say or feel. Anything that comes to mind should be written down until you have completely emptied out.

  During this process, let your emotions out too. If you want to cry, cry. If you want to scream, scream. Holding emotions in doesn't make them go away but it can leave you feeling like a balloon that is about to burst. Let a bit of air out so there is room to expand into again if needed.

- **Be kind to yourself**

  Like all of the work in this book, this is optional, but it's one thing I find very powerful. Do something nice for yourself. That could be as simple as taking a long, hot bubble bath, booking in for a massage, taking some time out for a walk. Something that you would label as self-care.

It can be easy to forget to look after ourselves when things get tough. I used to reach for the wine and takeaways during times of stress. I didn't feel like cooking and I wanted something to take the edge off and help me to relax but I only ever ended up feeling worse than before. Then I had the stressful situation to deal with, plus the lethargy that followed a period of indulging.

The better you feel, the better the situation will feel!

Controlling the Controllable

Let's talk about the 'what if' frame of mind. The 'what ifs' can lead you down a path that you probably won't thank yourself for. It's usually the road to feeling overwhelmed.

I almost found myself going there after I bumped into my hairdresser a few days after my visit to the doctor, whilst still waiting for my appointment to come through. The thought went through my head that if it was the worst-case scenario and I lost my hair, he wouldn't be cutting it for me anymore and I love my trips to get my mop chopped.

It was a fleeting thought and I caught myself very quickly so that I didn't spiral down a rabbit hole with no way out. I realised I was focusing on things that were outside of my control and what I didn't want to happen. When you do that, you will feel out of control.

This isn't limited to times of pressure or strain; this goes for life in general and spending time attempting to control things that are outside of their control is something that many people do every day. There are discussions day in and day out about the news and what has been reported that day and there is often a lot of emotion that goes with it. The reality is that there is very little, or probably nothing at all, that you can do about the government, the economy, other people, so trying to change those things is one way to feel out of control.

When I thought about my appointment, the results that will follow and how my parents would cope if I was sick, I felt completely overwhelmed about things I can do nothing about and may not even happen.

> *"I have spent most of my life worrying about things*
> *that never happened."*
> **Mark Twain**

Worrying about things you can do nothing about changes nothing, except the way you feel, which is everything. Trying to change things you have no influence over creates a mindset of defeat and frustration and it can lead to generalising the experience across other areas too. If someone is feeling frustrated that the price of holidays abroad has increased by 50% that year, and their energy is being used to complain about it, thinking about how wrong it is and focusing on what will happen because of it, this is totally disempowering. That frustration and the mentality that life is just happening and they have no control over it will most likely end up flooding into their life in many other ways too, from their workplace, their children's school, the price of grocery shopping, because we take ourselves with us wherever we go and the vibration we are emitting attracts more of it. Your RAS will look to bring you the things you focus on, whether they are wanted or not. That is when it really does become overwhelming!

There are some things in life that we may not completely be in control of, yet we can influence the direction they take. These are usually connected to the people we interact with closely and so therefore have the potential to make changes with along the way. That said, there are no guarantees, because we are not magicians capable of jumping into the minds of others and changing the decisions they make. This is again where a lot of people direct their focus when attempting to change circumstances in their life – spending endless hours trying to get their teenager to behave in a different way, their boss to manage staff with more compassion, their partner to eat more vegetables. This can sometimes work but if I was a betting person, I would say the odds are not going to be in their favour.

You may be wondering what you should focus on, because most things will always be outside of your control, and that is the whole point. Most external things in your life you will have very little, if any, influence over, so my recommendation is that you don't even bother. Feeling annoyed because you can't change something you have no power to change is a vicious cycle with no exit, and it uses a lot of energy that could be better spent elsewhere, working on the things you can control, the things that will actually make the biggest difference.

Let's say the price of holidays abroad does increase by 50% in a single year. Unless you are the one who decides the price of holidays, then it's outside of your control. One person could spend their time focusing on the problem and they're unlikely to come up with a solution when doing that. They won't have a holiday abroad and they won't feel good either.

Another person may realise the price is outside of their control and so choose to focus on what is within their control instead. They accept that a holiday abroad in their usual way is off the cards and so they look at what they can do instead. By doing this they may come up with other ways they could spend their summer that will give them the same fun, relaxation and family time they would've had on their holiday and, most importantly, they feel in control. They are choosing the direction of their life.

Letting go of what you cannot control gives you the capacity to get creative and feel empowered in any situation.

During the 2020 Covid-19 lockdown, I was a new business owner and so didn't qualify for any business support or personal grants from the government. At that time, I was running classroom-based training and so became unable to deliver my service in the usual way. This was one of the biggest tests of resilience I have ever had in my life. Not only was the newly created business model not able to function in the way I'd planned, I also had no income to support me over the period of adjustment I had to make. There were an exaggerated number of circumstances that were outside of my control. My partner and I had also just moved into a new property the month before lockdown and our outgoings had increased by some margin. My business was on track to do very well that year but, one by one, people were cancelling their courses. They were concerned about their own finances and being unable to work and so didn't want to pay for training that didn't appear like it would be able to go ahead, at least not in the way they had originally signed up for. My life felt overwhelmingly out of control. Up to that point, I'd always had the mindset that the worst-case scenario when it came to the business was that I could go and get a job and move to a smaller, more affordable property, which I was okay with. Suddenly, jobs were few and far between and any opportunity to move house had been taken off the table. There were no viewings. The world had come to a standstill.

I had to take a deep dive inside myself to pull out internal resources I didn't know I had and may not have ever been aware of if lockdown hadn't happened in the way that it did. I had to go back to the drawing board of everything I knew and pull out every tool in my toolkit to stay resilient and focused. My starting point was carrying out the activation point exercise below.

ACTIVATION POINT – *Creating Control*

This exercise will give you clarity about what you can control and where to put your focus. Keep it really simple.

- **Draw a circle on a page, then draw another around that circle and then draw another around that circle. In the outer circle write 'Out of Control'. In the middle circle, write 'Influence'. In the inner circle, write 'Control' (see image 3).**

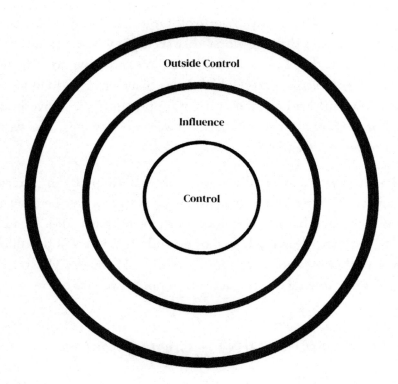

Answer the following questions.

- **What is outside of my control?**

  In the outer circle, make a list of everything that is outside of your control that you think about, feel any kind of emotion towards or even try to control.

  These are often the very things that keep people up at night and leave them feeling physically exhausted and powerless to make any positive shifts in their life.

  Some examples include the government, the weather, family, economy, opening hours of the gym, dress code at work, the traffic at 8.30am in the morning, the price of coffee.

- **What is within my influence?**

  In the middle circle, make a list of everything you have influence over.

  You may have access to the people involved or be able to assist and direct change in this area but it's not totally within your control.

  Some examples include your children, the hours your partner chooses to work, your work contract.

- **Finally, it's time to write in the inner circle. Make a list of all of the things that are completely within your control.**

  This may be a short list because there are many factors that are outside of our control and very few that are. That said, it may actually include things you hadn't even considered before.

  Some examples include physical well-being (diet, exercise, fresh air, staying hydrated, resting, quality sleep), mental well-being (who I spend time with, how I spend my time, my environment and how organised it is, meditation, taking time out, self-development, emotions), pin-pointing what specifically I feel emotional about so I know what is going on, talking with people, getting help and support where needed, focusing on what you can do right now.

When there are things that feel outside of your control, look for the things within them that are within your control, for example, finances. Whilst you may not have the money needed to cover things or pay off credit cards, one thing you can do is open up the lines of communication where needed. If you are unable to make payments when required, let people know and arrange an affordable payment plan in its place. These small actions add up to big movements and they are the very things that will allow you to sleep soundly at night.

Ignorance is not bliss! Pretending something doesn't exist doesn't make it disappear. When you face the things you need to deal with, you can then look at how you can overcome them and make a plan, even if you're not sure what that plan is to begin with.

The circumstances are what they are and you may not be able to change them but what you can change is how you choose to respond to them. The more control you have over your well-being, the more in control you will feel about everything.

I have carried out this exercise many times throughout the years and each time I have felt calmer and more able to deal with what is in front of me at that time.

Just before I close off this chapter, I can confirm that all was good and the lump was nothing more than a cyst. What a wonderful blessing in disguise it turned out to be.

Chapter 12
Lessons to Be Grateful For

"If you want to be happy, be."
Leo Tolstoy

One of the most spoken about practices when it comes to attracting the things you want is to practise gratitude daily. Something I did regularly, and whilst I understood the concept, my purpose for doing it was somewhat misguided.

When I first started my practice, I used to make a list of all the things I was grateful for each morning when I woke up and for a while it felt really good. That was until I noticed I was just saying the same things over and over again… my warm bed, a good night's sleep, plenty of food in the cupboard, a supportive and loving family, hot water, clothes to dress myself… The list went on. I was, of course, grateful for these things but I soon discovered I was practising gratitude from a point of lack rather

211

than abundance. Whilst on the surface being grateful regardless of where it comes from may seem like it's not a deal breaker, the feeling behind gratitude really does change the whole practice itself. Remember, you get what you focus on whether you want it or not, so that feeling of lack in my gratitude practice back then was only going to give me more lack. My practice had become more about settling for the things I had in life rather than really going for the things I wanted and it's something I've witnessed with others who use gratitude as a tool to enhance their life but end up creating the opposite effect. A client of mine experienced this very thing, which came to light early on in our coaching sessions. Many years ago, my client, who we'll call Sarah for confidentiality reasons, came to see me because she was feeling unfulfilled but couldn't understand why. She had a great life on paper and it bothered her that she felt like something was missing.

During one of our sessions, Sarah told me about her friend Jane who'd she'd grown up with in a small town. They were best friends and when they were younger, they enjoyed spending their time talking about the dreams they had for their lives. Their aspirations were big and exciting and they believed anything was possible. Sarah was a massive animal lover, who would stop to greet every dog she passed on her walk to school. She begged her parents to have a family pet, until one day they agreed she could have a hamster. If she proved she was responsible and looked after it, they would consider getting a cat. After six months of pouring her love into her hamster, who she named Mr Dominic, she was surprised and delighted when she came home to find a tiny little kitten waiting for her. Jerry the cat, named after the cartoon show Tom and Jerry, was soon following her around the house and cuddling her at night. Sarah made sure she fed, fussed and played with Jerry, along with cleaning out his cat litter tray every day. It was the final day of school before the summer holidays when Sarah's parents picked her up from school to take her to celebrate a year well done. She assumed they were heading to their local TGI Fridays, which was Sarah's favourite restaurant, so she was confused when they pulled up at the local animal sanctuary. Her parents led her inside and took her through to a room to meet the latest member of their family, a dog. Sarah burst into tears of joy. She ran to meet what would soon become her best friend and companion. She named him Ben. By this point she had found a fondness for Ben & Jerry's ice cream and so decided Ben the dog and Jerry the cat would make a deliciously amazing team. Ben was a stray who had experienced a lot of trauma, leaving him frightened to begin with. However, it didn't take long for him to open his heart and fall in love with Sarah and her family, just as they did him. Seeing the journey Ben had been through, from being rejected to being accepted, and how it had transformed him from a sad and lonely dog to being happy, fun and content, lit a fire within Sarah. She knew she wanted to become a vet and own an animal sanctuary to help animals without a home.

Jane had witnessed the passion Sarah had for animals right from the day her hamster, Mr Dominic, arrived and she enjoyed every second of watching her play with and care for him. There were so many wonderful moments and Jane felt an urge to capture them so the friends would be able to look back at them and remember those times in the future. That Christmas, she asked her parents for a camera so she could do just that. Jane's love of photography grew and before long her portfolio became a masterpiece of work that, in Sarah's opinion, would challenge even the greatest of all time. Jane had big goals to become a travel photographer,

213

travelling the world and capturing its wonders through her images.

Both girls were so passionate about their goals and ambitions and they were equally excited about each other's dreams and what they could achieve.

Both attended sixth form to gain their A levels. Sarah took a year out to earn some money before heading to university whilst Jane decided to bite the bullet and took a job abroad as a photographer's assistant. She saw this as the first step to pursuing her dreams. The next 12 months flew by. Jane demonstrated amazing ability in her role and ended up with a few of her very own clients. Meanwhile, Sarah had found herself a job where she happened to meet a really nice guy and fell head over heels in love. Her plans to go to university dwindled out. She didn't want to leave her new man right now; she was happy and her work paid reasonably well for her age, so life was good.

As the years went by, Jane and Sarah continued to keep in contact, either by email, phone or the odd meet-up. As time passed, those occasions became less frequent and their connection was mainly through liking each other's posts on social media.

A few years had passed when Jane dropped Sarah a message to let her know she was in the area and would love to meet. She couldn't wait to hear all about Sarah's life and what had changed since they last got together.

When they saw each other, there were lots of hugs, kisses and tears. They felt so comfortable together, just like they always had all those years ago. Jane began by telling Sarah all about the places she'd been, the people she'd had the opportunity to work with and the plans she had coming up. She showed Sarah some of her amazing photography and she was positively beaming.

After a lot of nattering, Jane shifted the focus to Sarah who immediately showed her the photos of the new addition to her family, a little cockapoo called Charlie. This prompted Jane to ask Sarah about her plans for university and her dreams to become a vet and have her own animal sanctuary. It was the first time in a while that Sarah had even thought about those plans. She explained to Jane that whilst that would be lovely, she had to be realistic. She had responsibilities and there were things she needed to take care of. Sarah had made the decision that she had to grow up and get her head out of the clouds because she had bills to pay. After her whirlwind romance, which eventually ended, she had found a new partner. They'd decided to buy a house together and so she needed to stay in her job until she had saved up a deposit. The job had become very mundane very quickly but she was doing it for a reason, so it was serving a purpose for her. At the time, she convinced herself it was only temporary and she would revisit the whole animal thing at a later date. Admittedly, it had gone on longer than planned but it was still just a stepping-stone to get her set up, ready to take the leap. Once she had a mortgage, then it would be the right time and she could consider her options.

It was another few years before they caught up again and updated each other on what they had been doing since they last met. Jane was now living in New York and travelling all over the world with her photography. She'd met a guy along the way and married him in a small beach ceremony six months earlier. They were going to take an extended honeymoon the following year, travelling around Europe. The great thing with Jane's work was she could do it from anywhere in the world and she loved it so much, she would do it even if it wasn't work.

Sarah then told Jane about her latest job, one she wasn't particularly enjoying but the pay was a step-up from the previous and it came with a promotion. This was good but it also meant she had more responsibility, so she was stressed a lot more often. All being said, it allowed her and her partner to go on holiday a couple of times a year, and boy did she need that! She now had the house she had been saving for, she was engaged, her wedding was fast approaching and in a couple of years they would probably start trying for a family.

Jane loved hearing Sarah's news. It appeared she had created so many of the things she wanted, but she was curious if Sarah still dreamt of becoming a vet and having her own animal sanctuary. It was something she had been so passionate about and her plan had always been to revisit it at a later date. It came as a bit of a surprise to Jane when Sarah looked confused by her question. She had completely forgotten all about her dream and Jane mentioning it was the first time she'd thought of it for quite some time. It had faded into a distant memory, a childhood fantasy. She had become so ingrained in the day-to-day of life that she rarely gave any thought to her dreams anymore. Those things had been put on hold a long time ago so she could focus on what she thought she needed in her life at that time.

What Sarah said left Jane feeling saddened. It was a story she'd heard many times before from the many people she'd met along the way.

Sarah told her the big things in her life were taken care of which, in her world, meant her mortgage, a pension plan and a husband-to-be – things most people would see as being big achievements, markers of doing well. She then added that she didn't need anything else, so she really should be grateful for what she has. She may not be a vet or have her own animal sanctuary but there were others who were way worse off. Whilst she wasn't happy or fulfilled in her job, it paid the bills, which was more than many people could say these days.

In the space of a few years, Sarah had gone from thinking about the wonderful life that she wanted – having her own vet practice and animal sanctuary – to the life she felt was necessary: having a mortgage, a good job, a pension, a life she was willing to settle for, a life where at least the bills were paid. She used the things she should be happy about by most people's standards as her reason to feel grateful, because life could be worse. Her gratitude was based on a comparison of other people's situations. Sarah reasoned that she had many things to feel grateful for: she could eat, she had her health, friends, partner, a warm bed, things that so many take for granted as being a given. This is very true as it's easy to lose sight of just how fortunate and truly wealthy a huge number of the population actually are today. Whilst you may not have the latest iPhone, just the very fact that we have the ability to make calls across the world at any time of day is just mind-blowing! We have the world at our feet and all the opportunities that come with it, and that really is something to be grateful for. But feeling blessed for the gift of where you are doesn't mean you shouldn't want more for yourself.

Gratitude is a beautiful and powerful practice and it's not about living from a place of, 'Life could be worse; I should just be grateful.' It's about taking time to appreciate the life you have and all the good things in it. It goes back to where you place your focus. When you spend time appreciating those very things, it's not just thinking it or saying it, you have to feel it, otherwise it's just words. I'm sure you've experienced a time when someone is saying the right thing but you just know they are not feeling it. It's the same with gratitude!

Life can be so busy and it can be easy to allow yourself to get pulled into the never-ending rat race and lose perspective on what matters. There is always something new to buy – the latest phone, car, pair of boots, gadgets, clothes – and as soon as you have them, a new, even better one comes out. Wanting better for yourself is a good thing; we all deserve the best and we're programmed to continually strive for more. It can become a problem though when there is no time spent appreciating what is already present in our lives. We take ourselves with us wherever we go, so no matter how many new phones or cars someone creates in their life in the future, if they don't appreciate the life they have right now, they won't enjoy the things that follow.

When you notice the abundance around you and focus your attention on it, your RAS brings abundance to your attention.

Stripping things right back is a great way to appreciate how much abundance you really have, abundance that is so often seen as a given. Taking the time to think about all the things that just happen for you every single day without thought – the kinds of things many only realise the value of once they are compromised or gone, the amazing miracles that take place every minute of the day.

When your health is not 100%, you realise how blessed you are to feel well.

If someone hurts you, you understand how good it feels when you're in love.

Being surrounded by people who drag you down heightens your appreciation for being with those who lift you up.

Experiencing something's opposite brings into awareness how fortunate and abundant you really are. Gratitude is learning to appreciate those things regardless, not just because they have been or could be taken away. Those positive things are always there and it's easy to become numb to their existence and forget how many wonderful things we have in our lives.

Like every emotion we feel, gratitude has a frequency to it and that frequency vibrates at a high rate. Focusing on what you appreciate in life requires focus and our conscious mind only has the capacity to focus on one thing at a time. This means that if you give your full attention to the things you feel grateful for, the other negative emotions will not be present in that moment. You cannot feel grateful and angry at the same time – the frequencies are too far apart from each other. If your focus is on one, the other does not exist in that moment. When someone is truly feeling the emotion of appreciation, the waves of their emotions, the vibrations and wave cycles are formed close together, which increases the speed your desired and positive manifestations come into physical form. Tipping the scales more in the direction of what is wanted, even if just slightly, will cause shifts to take place in favour of them.

A Test of Gratitude

Let's get real. Being grateful when things are good can be quite easy. The days where everything seems to go your way: you wake up on the right side of the bed, your hair falls into place, you miss the traffic, you open your email to a big order, someone pays for your coffee… Oh how lovely life is! Why wouldn't you feel grateful?

The real test of gratitude and the true meaning of it is putting it into practice when things are not so good, and these are also the times when it is most powerful. Being grateful for the things that on the surface cause the most pain has the power to shift the meaning you give to those experiences and change your whole perspective about them.

I personally went through a period during the 2020 lockdown, when things did not go well, along with many other people in the world. I used this time to really practice working on my focus. Don't get me wrong, I spent a good couple of days feeling really sorry for myself and I'm sure most people would've said I had every right to. I felt worthless, like I didn't matter, and completely powerless. In those moments, I did not feel grateful for an awful lot. The bits of gratitude that I lightly practised during the first few days were definitely coming from a place of lack. I remember thinking something along the lines of, *I'm grateful that I'm locked in and no one can see me because I can't afford to buy clothes anyway.* I allowed myself to live at effect, fully. I decided the situation I was in was causing me to feel bad and there was nothing I could do about it. I took no responsibility and so I couldn't do anything about it. This got boring very quickly! I was fed up of hearing myself moan, particularly knowing what I know. If I continued down that road, it was only going to get worse.

After the initial sting of not having any support from the government, I looked at where I did have support, both within myself and the support I had from others. I knew that, as I was fit and healthy, I could support myself physically to carry out whatever tasks were needed. I had my partner supporting me; he made me laugh every day. My parents were willing to move heaven and earth to make me feel good. My brothers would check in regularly and point out all the good things I had going for me. I had a lot of support and decided to focus on that.

When your head is the problem, it can feel like you have a metaphorical box on your head and it's easy to lose sight of everything else that is going on around you. Everything else includes all the positive things, of which there are so many. Even through the worst of times, there is always something, even if it's the smallest thing in that moment, that you can be grateful for.

Practising gratitude during the hard times is the most testing but also the most powerful personal tool. And when you do, it has the potential to change every challenging situation you ever face.

When those testing times come along, and they will, in those very moments, look for what you can be grateful for about the event, the struggle or the situation that is taking place. Find something to appreciate about the thing itself.

During lockdown I quickly began to appreciate the kickstart it gave us in our business to innovate and look at new and improved ways to work. This is something we probably wouldn't have done for years, if at all, had we not been forced to. Necessity is the mother of invention after all. I also appreciated that it reconnected me with nature. In the months prior to lockdown, I had been doing most of my workouts at the gym and getting less fresh air than I like to have. Taking a daily walk wouldn't have happened so often without it. With restaurants closed, I appreciated the new dishes that my partner learnt to cook. I'm not going to pretend I got involved in the actual cooking side of things, but I did enjoy eating them!

It was also the time that I had the inspiration to write this book, so without it, you wouldn't be here reading this today. That, I am truly grateful for!

The toughest times are the ones that give us the opportunity to grow the most. It's more common to only realise the benefits of a seemingly bad experience after the event. By seeking out the positive and looking for a reason to be grateful for it whilst you're going through it, you are one step closer to being the powerful creator you were born to be.

Lessons to Be Learnt

I hold it close to my heart that we have the opportunity to learn from everything we go through, everything we experience, both what we see as good and bad. There is always something positive we can take from it that will improve our lives in the future. When we choose to see everything as a chance to learn and grow, we are then able to view our experiences in a different light, knowing they have served us in ways we may not even be aware of until a later date.

Finding a lump left me reflecting and one of the first things I wondered was what I could learn from it. I quickly admitted to myself that I spend way too little time doing things that I enjoy outside of my work. I'm what many would label as a workaholic. I just see it as being passionate and determined and I know that to achieve the things I want takes more than working 9am to 5pm. I love what I do and I sometimes allow it to be all-consuming. What I have learnt is that there is no rush. I know my goals will continually grow as I do and so enjoying the other parts of life along the way is essential. I also know that my work will only benefit as a result of me being more rounded and whole as a person.

Events where there is no meaning found in the experience of them are the ones that will continue to have negative emotions associated with them, which makes perfect sense. When there has been a really difficult time in your life and the experience appears meaningless, it can leave you questioning what the point of it, or even life, is. When you are able to use those experiences to create a better future, you can more easily accept that they were part of the journey leading you to a life you would never have known about without them.

No matter where you are starting from, your current circumstances or what you are working through right now, there will be a positive lesson in there, even if it's one you have to go searching for.

When you ask the right questions, the questions you want the answers to, you activate your RAS to look for those answers. You direct the focus of your mind to give you the solutions you seek.

The important thing to remember is that knowledge is not power; it's the application of that knowledge that is powerful and it's the same when it comes to lessons. Understanding what you have learnt from a situation is only part of the story; it's about how you then use and implement the lesson to make positive changes in the future. From the things you have learnt, decide what you will do differently and take action towards doing it. Lessons are there to teach us and until we actually learn from them, we'll repeatedly come up against the same experiences. It may appear in different forms but the lesson itself will be the same.

For years I kept having situations come along whereby a significant person in my life would make a suggestion or a decision about what we should be doing and even though I wasn't sure about it or didn't think it was the right thing to do, I went along with it anyway. Almost every time, after things not working out, I proved myself right. I knew it wouldn't work but I did it anyway.

This included everything from whether to go on a second date with someone I had my doubts about, to taking a job that didn't feel right, to choosing which dress to wear on a night out. Each time I let other people's opinions determine the choices I made, even though they weren't what I thought was best, I would end up in the exact position I didn't want to be in.

I was completely oblivious to the fact that it kept happening, until one day when I found myself thinking, I've done it again!

That was when I took notice and recognised that this kind of thing has happened more than once, which is usually a sign that there is a pattern of behaviour going on. Remember that behaviour exists in your unconscious mind, so most of what you do day in and day out is outside of your awareness. Becoming consciously aware of a pattern is the first step to changing it.

I asked myself what it was that I was repeatedly doing that wasn't serving me. The answer came to me that I wasn't trusting myself. I argued with myself for a while, questioning whether or not I could or should trust myself. The irony! I kept coming back to the same conclusion: the times I hadn't trusted myself were the very times that things hadn't worked out.

The lesson was that I can and must trust myself.

There is a key component when it comes to really benefiting from the experiences you have and incorporating the lessons learnt and that is all to do with the direction of your focus that follows.

When we first learn something, it's often focused on the mistake that we don't want to make again. The issue with that is the direction of focus is then on what is not wanted or what you won't do in the future. Your unconscious mind processes the instructions you give it, whether it is about wanting it or not wanting it.

I knew I had to learn to trust myself, but if I'd have said, *"My lesson is that I shouldn't trust other people,"* all my unconscious mind would have registered is, *"Trust other people,"* and the lesson would never be learnt. It's vitally important that you take the lesson and make it a positive learning for you, and this is really simple to do.

When you know what you don't want or won't do, which is often related to other people, just spin it around and look for what you will do instead, something that will positively help you in the future.

For example, *"Rather than not trusting other people, I will trust myself."*

This will activate your RAS to focus on and bring into your awareness all the ways to do that very thing.

ACTIVATION POINT – *Learning Lessons*

Time to learn from your experiences.

- **What positive lessons can I take from the negative experiences I am going through or have been through in the past?**

  This is particularly relevant to events where there are still negative emotions present. Really consider how it will help you in ways that wouldn't be possible had you not had the experience.

  If you keep thinking the same thoughts when events occur, ask yourself the following question:

- **What am I not paying attention to that I need to?**

  Your unconscious mind will keep knocking on the door of your conscious mind until you answer. Listen!

  What are the thoughts that keep coming up that get pushed to the side?

Maybe you keep telling yourself you need to take time out but then you carry on regardless.

Could it be knowing you need to contact a certain person but you keep putting it off?

Pick up a blank piece of paper and write whatever comes to mind. Listen and trust yourself.

Turning Knowledge into Power

The important part then is integrating the lessons. As I already mentioned, only when you put those lessons into action will your unconscious mind stop giving them to you.

If you kept failing a driving exam with the same error each time, you wouldn't be given a driving licence. You also probably wouldn't just keep taking it over and over again, wondering why you're not passing. To be successful, you need to take the feedback on why you failed, learn from it and then apply those lessons. When you retake your driving exam using what you have learnt from your previous attempts, you are able to do it with new applied knowledge, which is power!

ACTIVATION POINT – *Applying Learnings*

Taking your answers from the previous exercise, ask yourself the following questions:

- **How will I implement the lessons into my life?**
- **What positive changes will I make?**
- **What will I do differently knowing what I now know?**
- **How will this benefit me in the future?**

  Make sure you focus on what you WILL do differently, rather than what you will avoid doing.

Chapter 13
Creating Magic

Think like the person you want to become.

You've made it to this point in the book and maybe you have put into practice all of the activation points; maybe you haven't yet. Either way, that's okay. You have already come so far. This book is here for you to use as a working manual that you can come back to any time and use whichever activation point you feel will serve you most.

Wherever you are right now is perfect!

You have learnt so much about how your mind works, how you create your reality, how you change your reality, the mechanics of physical manifestation and the power of focus. You also had an insight into how to create a mindset for success, how motivation works, getting through failure and the tough times and using gratitude as a tool to learn powerful lessons.

Now we're onto the magic of creation and I have to warn you in advance that what you are about to learn isn't rocket science! In fact, you have probably heard most of it a million times over already, and you may even be bored of hearing it because you know it.

I've also said this a number of times throughout this book, but it's worth repeating as this isn't limited to this book; it's about everything you have learnt, may know already or have read about in the past...

Knowing something doesn't change anything, you have to do something about it!

There are varying studies that show people have to digest information a number of times before it actually sinks in. This theory has been applied across advertising and marketing with what's known as the 'marketing rule of 7', developed by Dr Jeffrey Lant. The rule states that a potential customer must interact with a message at least seven times before they'll take action to buy it. Applying the same principle to your life, reading this right now could be the seventh time for you – the piece of the puzzle that makes it slot into place.

Whilst none of this is magic, if you apply it consistently, then it certainly can feel as if there is something magical taking place.

Let's get creating!

I'm going to break down each part of the creation process into really simple steps that you can easily follow to achieve anything you want in life, in any area of your life too.

Step 1: Discover Your Why

Find out your purpose, your reason for being here and for pursuing the things you want in the first place... Sounds big, right?

Where do you start?

A misconception that I used to have was that my purpose had to be a really big one that would have an impact on the whole world. I found this way of thinking put so much pressure on me that I was unable to think of a purpose grand enough to deliver on my expectations. When I realised that each and every person's purpose is different and the size of it is irrelevant, I was able to breathe a massive sigh of relief.

Your purpose is quite simply the thing that lights you up when you think about or do it.

This could be anything from creating delicious food for people to writing music, collecting antiques, sewing, sports, writing and everything in between. These are the things that make you feel fulfilled and even if you had all the money in the world, you would spend your time doing them anyway. Your purpose in life doesn't need to be a big, one-off, massive, life-changing thing that impacts hugely on other people; it's whatever lights you up, which will be something different to the next person.

A moment of enlightenment for me was realising that your purpose can change, and it will change as you do. Oh yes, your purpose is not a one-hit wonder that you must get right or you'll never live a fulfilled life. Your purpose when you are 20 will very likely be different to when you are 45 and have had more life experience, maybe some children and you're in a different phase of life. This is a good thing; it means we continually have potential to evolve.

It also doesn't always have to be career related. There are many ways your purpose can be achieved. Someone may have a passion for being creative and making things that brings joy to others and it's something they would happily do every waking hour. They could certainly set goals to create a business that allows them to do that, or they could find many other ways to do it. It could be something as wonderful as making candles and gifting them to people they love, restoring old furniture, or making beautiful accessories that leave women feeling wonderful, all of which could be a hobby or a career.

I once met a lady in the bathroom of a hotel who was smiling away whilst rubbing down the sinks. As we got chatting she told me how much she loved her work because her passion and purpose was to leave everywhere she went better and more sparkly than she found it. She decided to do this through her work as a cleaner and she loved every second of it. Her work may not have impacted millions of people and she probably wasn't considered as having big ambitious goals by most people's standards, but she loved her life and she was honest about what she wanted. This may have changed over the years or she could've found new ways to fulfil her purpose in a way that did impact more people and made an even bigger difference in her own life, or she may not have. The point is that she lived a life that filled her with joy, not one she believed looked good on paper to other people. Once you know what your why is in life, the rest will follow more easily. When setting any goals, keep your purpose in mind, checking whether they support it or take away from it.

If you are unsure or you want further help in discovering your purpose, head to www.iamsianhill.com/book-resources, where you'll find your free Discovering Your Purpose exercise.

ACTIVATION POINT – *Your Purpose*

- **Complete the Discovering Your Purpose exercise.**

  When you live life on purpose and with purpose, you have the ability to keep going when most would give up, because it's about something so much bigger than a goal.

Step 2: Know Your Outcome

What do you want?

It sounds so simple and it is, yet it's one of the most overlooked steps in creating what you want. Without clarity, the roadmap to get you there will be unclear and hazy at best. The more specific you are with your intentions and goals, the easier they will be to achieve.

YOU ARE ACTIVATING YOUR RAS!

Having a crystal-clear vision about where you are going gives a firm direction to your unconscious mind. This activates your RAS, the gatekeeper, which then decides what is relevant to your goals and what information is allowed into your awareness and what stays outside of it. Your unconscious mind will filter the external world around you and show you the easiest pathway to achieving the very thing you want. If you only have a vague idea about what you want, you miss out on the opportunity of bringing the very things that will get you to your destination into your conscious awareness.

Just like the satnav, whilst inputting a general direction is better than no direction at all, it doesn't guarantee where you will end up; in fact, nothing does. That said, being as specific as you can be about what you want certainly increases your chances of arriving there.

When I first started to learn that we create our own reality, I remember feeling concerned about shutting down other opportunities by being so focused on one outcome. I wondered if being so specific would actually stop me from noticing all the other things going on around me so I'd miss out on so many of them. Rest assured, this is not the case.

Having a laser-sharp focus on where your life is heading points the compass towards the direction you want to take it in. The purpose of this is to home in your attention and activate your RAS, bringing the external possibilities around you into your physical reality – something you can see, hear, feel, smell and taste. You collapse the waves of possibility into a wave of probability by observing that reality in your mind. That doesn't mean you will arrive at your destination in exactly the way you imagine, and the destination itself may turn out to be slightly different too. The focus will lead you to your outcome and it's important to have flexibility along the way, which goes back to letting go of success. If you had a goal to manifest a specific car in a particular colour and you do manifest that exact car, but the colour is slightly different, you have still achieved your goal. Many people get so hung up on the details of what they want, they forget to notice they have created the very things they set out to do.

The purpose of focus is not to discount anything that isn't that exact thing; it's to give you and your RAS clear instructions on where you intend to arrive. The universe will deliver what you ask for and it also has the bird's-eye view of your life. As human beings on planet earth, we don't have access to the bigger picture at play and the reasons why the outcome we achieve can end up being different to what we aimed for. If the ideal car you want to manifest is bright red and it looks amazing, shiny and vibrant but you don't know that the red colour fades very quickly in the sun, the universe could end up leading you to a different colour car, a car that is more in line with what you have asked for and will be better than what you asked for. Keep yourself open to receiving what you want or something better. If something different arrives, be curious about how it may serve you in an even better way than what you originally asked for.

Be open to the universe giving you what you want or something greater.

Take time to really think about what you want. It's important to be honest with yourself whilst you do this, rather than giving answers you think you should, or that other people want to hear, or choosing something you think you can easily achieve.

Setting outcomes based on what society says is the 'right path' won't necessarily be the right path for you. There is simply no way that every single person on this earth wants the same things from a formal education, followed by a secure job with good perks, a pension, marriage, kids, the house, holidays twice a year. The traditional route may be exactly what you want and it may not. Think about what YOU want!

If you don't know yet, that's okay too.

ACTIVATION POINT – Destination Clarity

Time to get clear!

Begin here if you're unsure what you want.

- **Make a list of everything you don't want. You'll probably find this will come to you with ease.**

  Take your completed list and ask yourself what the opposite of each point is.

  For example:

  Unwanted: *"I don't want to work 9am to 5pm every day."*

  Wanted: *"I want flexibility and freedom to work hours that fit in with the rest of my day."*

Once you know what you want, carry on.

- **What will life be like when you have those things? What will you see, hear, feel, smell, taste? What will it give you? Make it exciting!**

  The reasons to thrive need to be bigger and more thrilling than the reasons not to.

Get stuck into the detail about how your life will be when all of those great, positive things are here.

You can use the list below for some prompts to think about:

- **How do you spend your time?**
- **What do you do for work?**
- **What do you do for fun?**
- **Who do you spend your time with?**
- **What happens in a typical day for you?**
- **What kinds of things are you saying to yourself?**
- **How do you feel?**
- **How do you look? What clothes do you wear?**
- **How do you hold yourself?**

Always remember to keep it focused on what you want or will be doing rather than what you don't want or won't be doing. Your unconscious mind doesn't process negatives, so being clear on what you don't want turns your attention towards that very thing.

- *"I'm no longer in the job I don't like."*
- *"I don't eat junk food anymore."*
- *"I have stopped lying in in the morning."*

Change it to something positive.

- *"I am doing work I love.*

- *"I eat healthy and nutritious food."*
- *"I jump out of bed as soon as my alarm goes off and feel energised every morning."*

Step 3: Start with the End in Mind

Time to make a plan!

It was around 2014 and I had managed to get myself into just under £20k of debt with nothing to show for it. This is more common these days with student loans, finance options to pay for cars, furniture and pretty much everything else you could need over a long period of time. Unfortunately, I had none of those things! No education, no assets, not even a wardrobe full of clothes. I had spent years living beyond my means in an attempt to feel good about myself. It wasn't a lavish lifestyle; I just wasn't earning very much. I hadn't learnt how to budget and over time the nights out, the coffees here and there, something that needed fixing on my car… bit by bit, they added up.

I had dug myself into a hole that I couldn't see a way out of and I used not knowing what to do as the reason for not doing anything about it. When I thought about HOW to get myself out of debt, I felt totally overwhelmed. It was too big a jump from where I was in that moment and it didn't seem possible. I didn't really believe it could happen and so I convinced myself it wasn't worth getting started. I'd developed the mindset and belief that I'd got into so much debt, the damage was done, so I may as well carry on and do it properly.

This behavioural pattern was also present with my eating habits at the time. If I'd had one biscuit, I was having the whole packet and then some. I wasn't taking into account that for every biscuit I had and every penny I spent, I was digging a bigger hole to get out of. Every single choice we make matters, so even putting that last biscuit back is better than not, no matter how insignificant it may seem.

There was a turning point for me. A really simple question was asked that changed my whole thought process. It wasn't groundbreaking but it did make me consider that there could be another way to the one I was following. The question I asked myself was quite simply,

"What if there was a way I could pay off my debt?"

Like I said, not groundbreaking!

It was the first time it had occurred to me that one way to stay stuck was to do nothing, and although I wasn't sure how, maybe it was possible to do, even if it may take a little while. One thing I knew for sure was that I had to at least begin the process.

I knew what I wanted to achieve and I was very clear. The aim was to have paid off my debts within 12 months, a date that was a massive stretch for me back then. I had no idea how I would get there but I took the approach that if I aimed high, I was more likely to reach or even go above and beyond my expectations than if I aimed low. I started with the end in mind!

At this point, the steps to get there were a complete blur and even thinking about what they could be was too much. I found it overwhelming. In my mind, if I'd known what they were then I'd have done them already. To keep it simple, I broke it down into bite-sized chunks, which made the whole thing more achievable. I reverse engineered the figures and worked out where I needed to be in nine months, six months and three months to keep on track with the 12-month goal; three months was still a stretch!

It was then time to look at what the weekly, even daily, activities were that I had to carry out to reach that three-month goal. Even more important than that, I had to decide what the very first step was, the thing I could do right now to get the ball rolling.

When I thought about my finances, the way I felt could be described as out of control, so I decided the very first step was to take control. This meant getting a spreadsheet out and working out exactly what money I owed and to whom. Trust me when I say, ignorance is not bliss! Not knowing where I stood felt scary and even though I didn't particularly like what I saw on the spreadsheet, for the first time in a while I knew what I was facing, which made it possible to plan.

My income up to this point had been sporadic and unreliable. I was working as an actress, model, massage therapist and anything else I could turn my hand to. Some weeks I'd have the most amazing payday and then nothing of substance for weeks, even months, at a time.

I started by asking myself what I needed to do to achieve my goal, and although I had no idea how that was going to pan out, I'd set my intention and I was ready to do whatever was needed to get there.

*"The quality of your life is determined by the quality
of the questions you ask."*

Tony Robbins

I was at the start of something new, without the answers I was looking for. I began by asking myself the questions I wanted the answers to, the answers I wanted my RAS to be on high alert for.

ACTIVATION POINT – Quality Questions

When people feel stuck, unsure or uncertain about what to do, it can be easy to ask questions such as, *"Why me?"*, *"How can this be happening?"*, *"How have I got myself here?"*, *"Why do I always mess up?"*

STOP! If these are the questions you are asking, these are the answers that your mind will look to answer. Your RAS will allow in the information to show you how.

- **Become aware of the questions you are asking yourself.**

   These will often be unconscious and so you may not even be aware you're doing it. Grab a pen and paper and take some time out to make a note of the thoughts and questions that come to mind when you think about the goal, the problem or thing you want to change or create.

- **Change the script.**

   Decide which questions you would like answered. Imagine you have some Q&A time with the universe because you actually do, all day every day.

Those questions could be something along the lines of, *"How can I achieve this goal?"*, *"How many ways can I find to make this work?"*, *"Who could help me with this?"*

The better the quality questions you ask, the better-quality answers you'll get. This is such a simple shift that you can do immediately.

I implemented this simple, although not always easy, task from day one and my radar instantly began looking for ways to do the very things I focused on. It was only a few days later that I was contacted about a job working a few days a week with flexible hours and the pay was good. I'll be honest, had I not completed my financial spreadsheet I probably wouldn't have taken the job. I had always assumed that taking a job and not pursuing my acting work was a sign of failure and not trusting that things will work out. I thought the universe would just deliver the work I wanted – a common mistake!

When you set your intentions, you have to play your part and show the universe and your unconscious mind how serious you are about it. You have to demonstrate that you are willing to do whatever is needed, even the things that you may not want to.

I didn't necessarily want to work in an office but I'd decided I was going to pay my debts off and if working in an office was going to kick-start that journey, then that was what I was going to do. I meant business. That didn't mean I couldn't act as well; it did mean I could pay for the petrol needed to get to an audition and feed myself along the way.

The part-time work didn't cover everything needed but it was a big step in the right direction. I kept my focus on the outcome, making it exciting and as life-like as possible so that it was so real in my mind I could almost taste it. I imagined the very last thing that would happen when my goal had been accomplished. I mentally played through the phone call of me paying off my final credit card balance. I heard the conversation that would take place, the things I was saying to myself, the pictures I had in that moment and all the feelings of pride and excitement. I held onto that image every time I felt the urge to buy something I didn't really need. I checked whether spending that money was in line with my plans and I made the feeling of paying off my debts more exciting than the thought of spending money on short-term pleasures.

All very practical things so far, but when you take care of the practical, it makes room for the magic to happen!

I suddenly started getting more work, more acting jobs, more photoshoots and the most amazing thing was that they seemed to fall on days when I was available; they didn't conflict with each other and they paid well. Everything started slotting into place.

By taking the pressure off money by getting a job and making progress towards my goal, the negative emotions around it had disappeared too and I was able to open up the metaphorical door to everything that had been waiting for me. The resistance had gone and I allowed opportunities that had always been there to come into my awareness. My RAS filtered through the noise and there they were, ready and waiting for me to take. My acting work actually contributed massively to paying off my debts, win-win!

Just over nine months later, I had reached my goal and I was debt free, a dream that had seemed impossible!

ACTIVATION POINT – *Stepping-stones*

Get ready to make your plan!

You know what your end goal is. It's now time to get even clearer.

- **What date will I have achieved it by?**

  Be specific! Setting a goal to be achieved by the summer could be any month of summer in any year. Give your goal a date so you know when you are aiming for, for example, *31st July* (followed by the year).

- **Break it down into milestones.**

  Where will you need to be at the halfway point to make sure you are on track?

  Break it down further again to half of that and then the first month. Keep breaking it down until you end up with a list of fortnightly, weekly or even daily tasks that you can work on to get there.

  For example, a goal to become the sales manager in 12 months' time for a specific company may seem completely out of reach for someone, yet when they break it down, in six months they could have completed a management training course; in three months they could have begun taking on extra responsibility in their current role and exceeded their sales targets; in a month they may have completed an online sales training course. The weeks leading up to that could consist of them carrying out the sales training, connecting with the new company team on LinkedIn to build relationships, getting a new suit to step into the role they want to be in, getting a coach to deal with any limitations. If there are any mental or emotional blocks that will be a potential obstacle and prevent the end goal from happening, then working with a coach, specifically a mindset coach, is a great place to start.

There are so many ways to begin to create movement towards the goals and whilst you may not know exactly what you need to do or what the steps are to get you to your end goal, it's all good. One task could be to find out what the steps are, to book a call with someone who does know, to do some research, go on a course. Finding out what you don't yet know is a task in and of itself, yet be mindful of using this as a way of procrastinating. Make sure it's a quick process followed by action.

- **What is the very first step I will take to get started today?**

What is something you can do straightaway, like right now? The quicker you do this and commit to your goal, the better. It's easy to get stuck thinking about, talking about and writing about goals but without action, nothing happens.

You will get back what you put in, so saying you want something and then doing nothing about it emits a mixed frequency and so you achieve mixed results.

No matter how big or small the action is, it's a message to your unconscious mind that you're serious, that it's important and so your RAS will be alerted and bring into your awareness the next step to take. It metaphorically and almost literally lights up the path to show you where to go.

Take action as soon as possible!

Step 4: You Will Be Tested – Be Prepared

Setting goals is wonderful, but setting them is the easy part. Achieving them, on the other hand, is unlikely to be as straightforward as we expect. Things will come up; obstacles will get in the way; there will be detours you didn't even know existed before you started, and it's at these times that your resilience will be tested.

Giving up can seem like the easy option but if you've made the effort of taking the first step towards your goals, then you're already further along than so many people ever find themselves. It makes more sense to keep going than it does to start all over again with something new, only to hit the same walls again down the line.

Think of the challenges as opportunities to prove to yourself how much you want it. They are chances to become more, to step into your true power.

"Challenges are what make life interesting and overcoming them is what makes life meaningful."
Joshua J. Marine

Seeing the walls, the hurdles, the obstacles and the detours as an opportunity to grow gives them a whole new meaning. They are chances to build character, chances you wouldn't have had without the experiences that present themselves when you push yourself.

At first glance, a metaphorical wall can appear quite daunting if it's not something you've encountered before. Or, that wall can be your biggest adventure if you choose to see it that way. When you ask yourself how you can get around it, climb over it, find people to give you a leg up, build a bridge, knock it down, or countless other ways, your RAS will show you how to do it. It's about asking yourself the questions you want the answers to!

Mentally rehearsing can also be used in advance to plan how you will manage and get through the times where things are not so easy. If you know there are scenarios that could happen and they have the potential to slow you down or even stop you in your tracks, plan how you will deal with them if they do, how you respond if things go wrong or when the goal becomes really hard work, when the motivation is being tested to the full!

Visualising your life turning out how you want it to is of massive importance in directing your focus and activating your RAS and it won't always be straightforward getting there. No amount of positive thinking is going to take away the challenges that will come up.

The saying 'what doesn't kill you makes you stronger' is true. When you're pushed to your limits, even if those limits are relatively small in comparison to other people's or even other areas of your own life, you have to grow in order to meet and overcome them. It's a mental and emotional workout that leaves you with more strength and flexibility when you get to the other side.

If the goal is to write a book by a certain date, then you will have to do some writing. The task of writing may well feel easy when you're inspired on a Tuesday morning after a good night's sleep, but what about a Friday evening, when you're feeling tired and not in the mood? What if your diary is packed with day-to-day obligations so the only writing time available is at, say, 5am on a Saturday morning?

If the goal is to lose weight, what will you do on a sunny Saturday when your friends are having a cold glass of prosecco and nibbles in the garden and you're meant to be heading to a spin class?

If you want to create more financial abundance, how will you handle it when an unexpected bill comes in, or you don't yet have the money to pay for something you want that month? How will you stay on track when things come up? And they will.

Temptation to give in or give up will present itself and usually quite soon after setting your intentions. It's your unconscious mind checking to see how serious you are about it. It's a test! You could liken this to a test that I've seen many people do in their relationships. Not that I'm saying this is something to do or I agree with, it's just a useful analogy to explain how it works. In a relationship when one person isn't certain about the commitment the other has said they will make, they may push them to test that commitment. They might give them an opportunity to get out and take a different path; they might push them away to see if they take it. If that person sticks around, it shows they are serious and committed to making the relationship work. Again, I'm not recommending this as a method to test your relationship in any way.

On the flipside, this also happens for the individual themselves. After starting a new relationship, there may well be other offers, or people, landing on the table, metaphorically of course! The reason for this is two-fold: firstly, that person is emitting a different vibration of 'being in a relationship' and so the possibility of relationships become more evident in ways they may not have seen before. And then there is the test. It's a check to see how serious that person is about the one they have committed to, and this is really useful to have!

The universe operates in the same fashion, so expect to feel tested.

This commonly plays out as other opportunities presenting themselves or the thing you are letting go of in order to achieve the goal you have set is suddenly there, ready and waiting.

I was tested when we first set up our company. Although I'd done different work over the years, I'd always stayed on the books for the agencies where I received my acting and modelling jobs. A few weeks after committing to the business and setting goals for it, agreeing to myself that I was all in, I was inundated with offers of work. I'll be honest, at the time, it was a hard test. That work was familiar to me and whilst it didn't satisfy and fulfil me, the work was good fun and there was money involved. For a while, I did question whether this was a sign that I should stick with that career. That was until I remembered there will be a test!

I see this a lot. People will begin taking steps towards something new and then the thing they are leaving behind suddenly gets traction and they see it as a sign to stick with it. I have been there, asking myself if the universe is showing me that I should stay with what I already do. Whilst this is never black and white, because nothing really is, in order for you to let something new in, you have to let go of something else to make space for it. If your focus is diluted and there are mixed messages running through your unconscious mind, then it won't know which way to turn. Your RAS may then miss the opportunities to make the new thing work because, in that moment, your focus is on continuing with the old thing.

When a test comes along, use it as a powerful gift that gives you so much information. If it isn't something you really want, this is the time you will know about it. Think about the relationship that is tested – if someone wants out, they will see this as the opportunity to do that and jump at it. Before making any decisions, check if you're exiting because you really don't want it or because there are limiting beliefs about whether or not you can achieve it, any limiting beliefs, negative emotions conflicts or things that need to change that are giving you an excuse to get out rather than dealing with them. Remind yourself of the goal you set and check if the offer on the table is working towards it or not. It is also an amazing opportunity to build your mental muscle. When you get through the test and stay committed to and focused on the goal you set, you come out the other end feeling so strong and in alignment, which can often be followed by a period of momentum. Your commitment pays off and focuses your RAS even more.

Keep in mind that your unconscious mind will always look for the easiest route to achieving everything, which again is where your RAS comes in – it seeks to find the path of least resistance.

Preparing in advance for these events, the tests, the obstacles, the times that can feel like a struggle, means that even when they do show up, you'll have practised them in your mind, seen yourself coming out the other end and you'll feel ready to deal with them.

ACTIVATION POINT – *Operation Preparation*

When beginning this process, you can draw on past experiences you know have been an issue for you or experiences you have not had but could imagine taking place.

- **Make a list of any obstacles that could present themselves.**

  Write whatever comes to mind.

  For example, when it gets close to the end of the month and I have little money left over, I go into panic mode and completely forget about focusing on abundance. All my efforts go out the window and I begin focusing on lack and scarcity.

- **Go through your list and imagine that scenario happening and notice how you feel.**

  Ask yourself if you feel equipped to deal with it. If so, it's something you know you'll be able to handle – amazing!

  If not, carry out the following mental rehearsal process.

  Pretend for a moment that you are observing that very thing taking place and there is a chance for growth to happen. See yourself in the picture of your mind whilst it's taking place.

  As you do, imagine how it would play out if all went well. Even with the issues, you get through it easily and became a stronger person because of it.

  Then, step into your body in the picture, so it's as if you are really there, looking through your own eyes. Pay attention to how it feels to be the person who finds solutions because you know, deep down, there is always a way when you look for it. You know how your RAS works; you trust it and so as long as you focus on what you want, you know it will deliver the route to get there.

  See the world through your new eyes; hear the sounds around you, the words you say to yourself, the feelings and the knowledge you have.

  Then, allow that positive feeling to double in intensity and just sit with that new, positive, powerful feeling for a moment.

Take a deep breath in…

Now, check in with yourself and notice how those old hurdles feel different.

Imagine a time in the future when they could happen. Whereas in the past you wouldn't have known how to get around them, now you know you can.

You are able to step around them and keep moving forwards with the knowledge you have gained because of them. Something that will only ever serve you well in the future.

> *"Do not pray for an easy life,*
> *pray for the strength to endure a difficult one."*
> **Bruce Lee**

Chapter 14
Practice Makes Perfect

Knowledge is of no value
unless you put it into practice.

Before you come to the end of this book, I want you to know that you already have a good enough understanding of the mechanics of your mind to start making massive positive changes. There is so much more to dive into when it comes to your internal world and I encourage you to continue your journey of self-discovery whilst you put into practice what you have learnt so far.

It's all too easy to use learning and information gathering as the reason to delay putting things into action, but one thing I can guarantee is that no amount of knowledge will ever change your reality. You have to put what you know into practice.

I could tell you all day long about how to ride a bike but the quickest way to learn to ride is to do it. You may have stabilisers to begin with. You will probably fall off a few times, maybe even hurt yourself, but falling off is never the issue; the issue is staying off when you fall. Every time you climb back on that bike, you will have learnt something new, usually what doesn't work and how not to do it, yet without that experience, you wouldn't have known. And it's the same with life.

I spent years reading the theory behind manifesting my dream reality, getting the latest books, watching the latest YouTube videos, looking for the secret. The bit I'd missed was that I could read about it all day long, but if I didn't put into practice what I was learning, I may as well have not read it. Blaming the books, the videos and other people who are living the life you desire for not having what you want is the quickest way to feeling frustrated and getting nowhere!

This really is just another way of procrastinating from doing the very things you need to so you can truly move the dial in the direction you want to go in. If you wait until you have enough knowledge, enough time, enough confidence, enough money, you will be waiting forever. When your RAS is activated to find ways to delay and put things off, it will help you to find them.

The best way to get ready is to get started before you are ready, because the truth is that it's the only way. No one is ever ready to ride their bike without stabilisers and if you were to sit and think through all the possible outcomes, all the things that could go wrong when you finally kiss those two little pieces of metal goodbye, you'd be frozen with fear.

The first time I took my stabilisers off, I pushed away from the kerb and began peddling, slowly at first and then more quickly, and I soon realised that going that little bit faster gave me momentum. When going slowly, I struggled to balance and I found myself overthinking every move I made. As soon as I allowed myself to trust that I would work it out and gained just a little more speed, the forward motion seemed to keep me upright and I was able to ride easily.

Much like riding a bike, the more you hesitate, the worse it feels and the harder it is. Holding back won't serve you. It's like slowly lowering yourself into a freezing cold swimming pool one limb at a time – oh so painful! Holding onto the warm air outside of the cold water only makes you long to stay comfortable, even if what you really want is to have fun in the pool. Whereas when you dive straight in, it's uncomfortable at first, maybe even a little painful for a second, but you soon get used to it. Letting yourself just go with it, fully immersing yourself and trusting that you'll be okay, allows it to happen.

You won't ever know if something is going to work beforehand and, in reality, if everything in life was guaranteed, it wouldn't be half as much fun. The challenge and achievement are what makes it worthwhile, even if it doesn't feel that way at times. The energy of being half in and half out has a mixed frequency to it because you are literally sending out mixed messages.

"I want it…"

"I don't…"

"But I do…"

"I'm not so sure…"

This will lead to things coming and going, like when you start getting somewhere and then it slows down. This kind of energy is palpable in relationships. When a person seems fully in one minute, then pulls back the next, it leaves the other person involved feeling confused and unsure about how serious they are and so they don't know how to respond. Commit to yourself fully – you deserve it!

ACTIVATION POINT – *Clear Message*

Think of the universe as your lover! The message you put out there is quite literally the vibration you are sending into the universe.

- **How clear are you about what you say you want? Are the messages you give to your unconscious mind, and therefore the universe, consistent or changing?**

  Notice if there are times when you think, feel or act in a way that is opposite to what you want.

  If there are, continue with the following question:

- **If I did achieve the things I really want, what would happen? What will change that I feel uncomfortable about?**

  Any uncertainty that we feel is there to protect us, even if the results it produces don't actually give us the life we desire.

Acknowledging that things will change and considering how that will impact on you in all areas of your life is important. Not paying attention to the things we fear or unconsciously pushing against them can leave us in an endless loop or conflict of wanting something but fearing it at the same time. This exudes an incongruence in our vibration and energy, leading to variable results.

- **If that change happened, how would I deal with it? What could I do to make it work?**

Acknowledging that any doubts, fears or conflicts all have a positive intention at their root will help you to see them in a new light, so you can be kind to your unconscious mind for doing its job. Beating yourself up and criticising yourself only hinders your progress. Your unconscious mind is like a five-year-old child, so treat it in the same way – with compassion and love. The more love you give, the more you get back and the better you will feel in the process.

Chapter 15
A Message from Me

A place that holds your hand
and guides you through each day
A world with every answer,
always showing you the way
A feeling you've come home,
yet you'd never really gone
Because you are it and it is you,
everything is one.

Writing this book has been such a privilege to do and a real learning curve for me personally. It has been a continuous reminder of just how powerful we are and how we really do have the ability to shape our realities when we are willing to do the work.

Whatever you want to create in your life, just know that you are already enough.

When the day comes to leave your physical body, which is one thing that is guaranteed in this life, no amount of money, cars, fame, the latest technology or toys will mean anything.

Approach everything you do for the joy brought in getting there. Have fun with the creation process. Enjoy seeing your progress – the evidence that presents itself to you, showing you're on the right track, no matter how small. The experiences you have along the way are what it's all about, so celebrate them. Celebrate being you.

If you don't enjoy the journey to the destination, the destination won't be enjoyable!

Your RAS is ready and waiting to serve you; let it be your best friend.

Finally, and most importantly, I mean this with all my heart, thank you for taking the time, your precious time, to read this book. I truly hope you have found some valuable insights and it will be a stepping-stone in the direction of creating your world, from the inside out!

Resources

Head to the website below to access resources, including the 'My Purpose Exercise' and 'Activation Point Exercises', found throughout the book:

www.iamsianhill.com/book-resources

If you would like to find out how you can work with me further, head to my website:

www.iamsianhill.com

Bibliography and Recommended Reading

Allori, Valia, 'Quantum Mechanics and Paradigm Shifts', *Topoi*, 32/2 (2015), 313–323

Bandler, Richard and Grinder, John, *Frogs Into Princes, Neuro Linguistic Programming* (Moab, UT, 1979)

Bandler, Richard, *Using Your Brain for a Change* (Moab, UT, 1985)

Braden, Gregg, *The Divine Matrix: Bridging Time, Space, Miracles, and Belief* (1st edition, Carlsbad, CA, 2006)

Dispenza, Joe, *Becoming Supernatural: How Common People Are Doing the Uncommon* (Carlsbad, California, 2017)

Dispenza, Joe, *Evolve Your Brain: The Science of Changing Your Mind* (Deerfield Beach, FL, 2007)

James, Tad and Woodsmall, Wyatt, *Time Line Therapy and the Basis of Personality* (2nd edition, Carmarthen, 2017)

Krasner, A. M., The Wizard Within: *The Krasner Method of Clinical Hypnotherapy*, (Santa Ana, CA, 2001)

Three Initiates, *The Kybalion: A Study of the Hermetic Philosophy of Ancient Egypt and Greece* (Chicago, IL, 1908)

Gribbin, John, *In Search of Schrodinger's Cat* (1st edition, London, 1985)

Sage, Peter, 'The Art of Living in Through Me', YouTube, uploaded by The Real Peter Sage, July 2016, www.youtube.com/watch?v=fJ4PB6YVjxY

Stark, G., 'Light,' *Encyclopaedia Britannica*, 1 December 2021, www.britannica.com/science/light

Acknowledgements

Writing a book has been an experience that has challenged and stretched me in so many ways and it wouldn't have been possible without the support of my wonderful mum and dad. Firstly, I have to thank my mum for being my sounding board, initial proofreader, researcher, basically an unpaid employee who wore many hats. Thank you so much for doing anything I asked without question. Then, my dad who, even through his own health struggles, always looked for ways to support me, taking away everyday tasks so I could focus on writing and always offering to help. You have both been a constant tower of strength, cheering me on and believing in me every step of the way.

Thank you to my partner, Dan, who always encouraged me to do the things I want, even though it meant I spent many evenings tucked away writing. You have always had absolute certainty that I can achieve anything I dream of and, no matter how hard or serious things have seemed at times, you have made me laugh along the way and seen the lighter side of life. I'd also like to thank Dan's mum, Ljiljana, who has been enthusiastic since day one, insisting that I push myself. Your eagerness and belief in me have been really wonderful.

Thanks to my friends and students who have spent the last couple of years asking me when they can have a copy of the book. Your enthusiasm to get your hands on it kept me going when it would've been easier to shut the laptop. I want to give a special mention to my wonderful friend Jemma Heaven for reading my first few chapters from the first ever draft, back when I decided I was going to write it and had no idea what I was doing. Even with a small baby and another one on the way, you took the time to read those initial pages and give me feedback. I'll always remember you saying to me, "It's like a real book," which I took as confirmation that I could do it, even if I wasn't sure how at that point.

A big thank you must also go to my editor, Jessica Kate Brown. Aside from the services you provided to bring the book together, you have given so much guidance and support, answering questions I didn't know I had, holding my hand through every step and being flexible with my ever-changing timelines as I worked through it. You were the first person to read the first full draft from start to finish and the feedback you gave me convinced me that the book was worth sharing.

I would also like to acknowledge and thank my teachers and leaders within the field of personal transformation, many of whom I have not had the pleasure of meeting, yet have had a profound impact on my life. Without the knowledge you have given me, this book would not have been possible.

About the Author

Sian is an internationally certified trainer of neuro linguistic programming (NLP), Time Line Therapy®, hypnotherapy and a master coach. She has worked with hundreds of individuals, through one-to-one coaching and training programmes where she has accredited coaches worldwide, teaching them the skills to change their mindsets, improve their lives and help others to do the same.

You can connect with Sian via her website:
www.iamsianhill.com

Instagram: @iamsianhill

Podcast: Vibrant Mind Vibrant Life

Printed in Great Britain
by Amazon

19974635R00156